Surviving Domestic Violence

Voices of Women Who Broke Free

Surviving Domestic Violence

Voices of Women Who Broke Free

Elaine Weiss, Ed.D.

Clinical Associate Professor
Department of Family and Preventive Medicine
University of Utah School of Medicine

Surviving Domestic Violence:
Voices of Women Who Broke Free
by Elaine Weiss, Ed.D.

Produced by the Department of Family and Preventive Medicine
and published by Agreka™ Books.

Publisher's Cataloging-in-Publication
(Provided by Quality Books, Inc.)

Weiss, Elaine, 1947-
    Surviving domestic violence : voices of women
who broke free / by Elaine Weiss. -- 1st ed.
    p. cm.
    Includes bibliographical references.
    LCCN: 99-91265
    ISBN: 1888106964

    1. Abused wives--Biography. 2. Abused wives--
Psychology. 3. Wife abuse. 4. Conjugal violence.
I. Title

HV6626.2W45 2000   362.82'92
                            QBI99-1510

Cover art Susan Makov
Cover design Bryan Baker

800 360-5284
www.agreka.com

Contents

Section I Why Don't They Just Leave?

Section II Getting Out

Section III After It's Over, It's Not Over

Section IV Letting Go. Going On.

Dedicated to the memory of Heather Belsey

September 21, 1968 – October 7, 1998

Foreword

It took just one phone call to shatter our illusions. The newspaper reported that the man called 911 and said, simply, "I killed my wife."

As a physician and professor in a medical school, I have known many people as they died. But the man's wife, Heather, was my first student to be killed in an act of domestic violence. Never again could my colleagues, our students, or I imagine that domestic violence happens only to someone else. It tore away one of our best.

Not a week before the phone call, Heather joined the group I led in the medical school's second year interviewing course. Each student took the medical history of an actor "patient." All of us then analyzed the videotape of the encounter. I vividly remember Heather's interview. Tall, bright-eyed, relaxed, she leaned forward to focus on her patient. Her caring and eagerness to serve filled the room. None of the rest of us imagined the danger she would soon face at home.

Yet just the day before, Heather and her classmates had listened to their first lecture on domestic violence. Had any of her fellow students seen hints of violence in Heather's life? Was the brutality that would kill her the first such overt act in her home? Sitting in the lecture, did she recognize herself in the stories of other women's pain from domestic violence? Was she stiffened by aches from flung words…or fists? If her professors or classmates been more alert to signs of fear, would Heather be alive today?

We will never know. What I do know, though, is that those of us who appreciated, respected, and loved Heather will never again think of domestic violence in the same way. Domestic violence is common. It is most often, though not always, directed against women. It can be fatal. It is something that many people have trouble comprehending, trouble recognizing, and trouble addressing. Physicians, like many people, may not know how to respond sensitively and effectively to domestic violence.

It is also true that many women in danger, like Heather, don't speak about their problem. Domestic violence is far more than just physical trauma caused by a loved one. Rather, those living with domestic violence find themselves caught in a prison whose bars grow invisibly but no less powerfully than steel. These bars come in shapes that are social, economic, emotional, intellectual, and physical. The woman caught in domestic violence may literally risk her life when she tries to break free. We'll never know Heather's true story; the extent to which she suffered in the weeks and months before her death. We only know that her death deprived us of a woman who had been on her way to becoming an outstanding physician.

Fortunately, Elaine Weiss and the women she interviewed have now stepped forward to tell us about their experiences. They tell of fear, strength, and courage. Their stories are painful…even searing. Yet whether you are a woman experiencing domestic violence, a friend or family member, a health, law enforcement, or legal professional, or even someone recovering from having injured someone you love, reading these stories is worth the effort. Each women whose story appears in this book is at a different stage of her journey. Each shows us that domestic violence need not be a death sentence, that women can indeed remove the prison bars one at a time and eventually break free.

So together, the women of this book have woven a new image: a story of hope, a path of inspiration. If this book helps prevent the death of even one person from domestic violence it will be worthwhile. But I think these stories will do far more. They will help many people reclaim their lives from the disaster of domestic violence.

It is my prayer that hearing women who have survived domestic violence will inspire others to begin their own journeys. Because of Elaine Weiss and the women who shared their stories with her, the rest of us can learn to reach out and help along the way.

Michael Magill, M.D.
Professor and Chairman
Department of Family and Preventive Medicine
University of Utah School of Medicine

Introduction

Humans are storytelling creatures preeminently.
We organize the world as a set of tales.
— Stephen Jay Gould. *Questioning the Millennium.*

This is not a reference text about domestic violence. It is not an instructional manual on how to escape from a batterer. Plenty of these exist. It is a travel guide to a country no one visits willingly, the collective tales of past travellers making the landscape less threatening, less alien.

People have always counted on stories to make sense of their lives. In 1997 I set out to gather a particular set of stories. I traveled across the country interviewing women who were once in an abusive relationship, who left their abuser, and who went on to reconstruct their lives. It was far too easy for me to find these women. I met them everywhere: on airplanes, at conferences, in community board meetings, at religious services, in offices, schools, and hospitals. Their stories were difficult to hear. Ultimately, though, the pain of the stories was balanced by the humor, insight, and remarkable courage of the women who shared them with me.

To grasp the full reality of domestic abuse, it must be approached, like a piece of sculpture, from multiple vantagepoints. No set of bare statistics, let alone the flat sound bites our society has come to call news, can capture its complexity: "Woman Knifed by Estranged Husband." "Lovers' Spat Ends Tragically." "Ex-Boyfriend Shoots Mom, Kids." We shudder, then quickly turn our attention elsewhere. As we avert our eyes, we assure ourselves that these dreadful events have no relevance to our lives.

An old folk tale describes a conversation between Truth and Story. Truth complains that her messages are not heard; when people see her, their eyes slide away. Story replies, "You are naked, ugly, and old. Although I am as old as you, I am well dressed and pleasing to the eye. People do not turn from me. They welcome me into their homes, they listen to my many voices, and they come to see for themselves what is true." I hope the many voices in this book will convince you that these stories belong to all of us. Domestic abuse doesn't just happen "out there" somewhere — it happens in our town, in our neighborhood, on our street. It happens to people we see at the supermarket, the movie theater, the ballet, the bowling alley, and the PTA board meeting. It happens to our friends, our coworkers, and our family members. Women who have experienced domestic abuse look just like everyone else. They look just like me.

Abused women also look just like Jesusa Fox, who currently lives in a Salvation Army halfway house. A devout Catholic from the Philippines married to an ex-Marine, she was able to escape from her husband only by making the unendurable decision to leave her two sons behind. Her husband has threatened to kill her if she fights for custody; nevertheless, she is determined to get the boys back.

Abused women look just like Judy North, a first-grade teacher from Nebraska who remained with her abusive husband for ten years, until the night she finally stood up to him…and woke up in the emergency room.

Abused women look just like Whitney Benson, a Mormon college student from southern Utah. She worries about the scars on her face from her boyfriend's class ring; I worry about the scars on her soul from his carefully crafted campaign of criticism, intimidation, and punishing rape.

And abused women look just like Andrea Hartley, a pediatrician in her late forties who considers herself extremely fortunate. Although the man she married when she was thirty proved to be extremely violent, the emotional support of her family, friends, and medical colleagues enabled her to leave him only four months later.

At first glance, the women who shared their stories with me appear to have little in common. They come from all walks of life. Some are well educated; others barely finished high school. Some come from wealthy families; others come from poor ones. Some witnessed terrifying family violence as children; others never heard an angry word. Some were raised by warm, supportive families; others by cold, distant families. Some married young; others married late. They worship in churches, in synagogues, or not at all. They come from big cities, small towns, farming communities, and suburbs.

What these women have in common is that each was in an intimate relationship with a man who abused her. Some were abused physically. Some were abused sexually. All were abused psychologically...the most devastating type of abuse, leaving the deepest wounds. Their stories only occasionally blaze with the dramatic pyrotechnics of afternoon talk shows. This is not a book about guns, knives, emergency rooms, or police reports. Many stories focus instead on the subtle campaign of abuse, wearying and corrosive, which trapped their teller in a web of daily threat. Yet despite the humiliation, fear, and isolation, each woman managed to escape from her abuser. Theirs are stories, not of frailty, but of clarity, resourcefulness, and strength.

What these women have in common is an aftermath: a word derived from the Old English "after-mowth," the second growth or crop. Like the grass that springs back after mowing, the feelings of shame, self-blame, helplessness, and blind fury reappear; sometimes as nightmares, sometimes as flashbacks, triggered by news reports, books, or movies. A woman who has been battered is never the same woman she was before it happened. Her history becomes woven into the fabric of her being. This should come as no surprise; it is equally true of a woman who has endured breast cancer, a woman who has given birth, a woman who has been widowed after loving and being loved long and well.

What these women have in common is their determination to reconstruct their lives. They have all spent time and energy struggling to understand, to draw meaning from the abuse. We believe we've made progress by calling these women "survivors" instead of "victims." And they are survivors, in the sense that their survival — their ability to not only function, but to prosper — is worthy of note. But in calling them survivors, we lose sight of the fact that they were once simply people. Little girls. Teenagers. Women.

What these women have in common is this. "You mean to say he beat you up? I never would have put up with that crap from my husband. You should have just left." As if the pain of domestic violence weren't enough, this smug pronouncement insists — and often convinces them — that this pain was their fault. Asking a woman why she didn't leave her abuser makes about as much sense as asking a victim of food poisoning why she didn't walk out of the restaurant that served her a dish of tainted salmon. Nevertheless, because the question is always asked, it must be answered. Each woman whose story appears in this book had her own reasons for staying. These will be addressed, examined, and — I fervently hope — put aside for good.

While the women whose stories appear in this book are courageous, they are not unique. Many other women have equally powerful stories. Many women escape from abusive partners, although it often takes years. Those who do not leave are no less courageous. Any woman in an abusive relationship, whether she has remained or managed to get free, is a strong woman. She has to be strong…to survive the daily assault on her character and human dignity. If you are currently in an abusive relationship, it must seem that there is no way out. The women who tell their stories here felt the same way. And then, somehow, they reached a turning point and they knew that they actually did have (in fact, had always had) the power to break free. As you read these stories, you will see that each individual woman's turning point was different. Perhaps this book will be the turning point for you.

Writing this book has taught me that stories can be gifts. For years I hid the story of my abusive first marriage. I was ashamed that I had allowed such ugliness to happen. I was embarrassed that I didn't "just leave." I worried that friends and colleagues who knew me as a strong, self-assured woman would think less of me. Then in 1994, inspired partly by the misunderstandings and noise that surrounded the murders of Nicole Brown Simpson and Ronald Goldman, I took a risk. I wrote an essay that described my own experience. When the essay was published in a local magazine, the response astonished me. I received letters, telephone calls, and e-mail messages from people in my community telling me that I had also written about them — or their sister, their mother, their daughter, their next door neighbor. The essay then seemed to take on a life of its own. Friends sent it to friends in other cities. Battered women's shelters across the country asked for permission to use it in their support groups. An international women's organization posted the essay on its web site. Another version of the essay was published in a national magazine. This resulted in even more letters. Not a week goes by without at least one e-mail message that begins with words like these: "I read your essay. I know what it's like to live with an abuser." The more I heard, the more I realized what I should have understood long ago: that there were many other women like me, women who broke free. As a writer, I could give voice to their stories, setting each down in such a way that its unique heartbeat could be felt.

I do so with the full understanding that any story imposes a burden on the listener. Stories demand as much as they give, because listeners are integral to the storytelling process. Listening to stories is not a passive act. The listener becomes the story, and so the story lives on. Nowhere is this more evident than at the Holocaust Museum in Washington, DC. The museum's goal is to tell the stories of the millions of Jews, Gypsies, homosexuals, artists, musicians, actors, and others who perished during this deliberate campaign of mass murder. Millions have visited the museum since it opened in 1991. Many come for intensely personal reasons: the friends and relatives who died in ghettos, prisons, and death camps. Many others come simply to learn. Everyone who visits the museum comes away shaken and wiser.

My friend Jane, who was raised in an Indiana farming community and met her first Jews when she started her freshman year at the University of Michigan, was no exception. All her life she had imagined the Jews of Europe dressed in rags, hiding in attics or creeping fearfully through desolate ghettos. Of course. These are the images the world has seen for years. But in the museum, she saw photographs of children playing violins. Fathers standing proudly beside sons. Families on a summer picnic. Looking at those photographs, Jane finally saw the Jews of Europe as people, rather than as victims. People much like her family in Indiana. And in that instant, she understood the full horror of the Holocaust.

Any horror — war, famine, disease, rape, poverty, abuse — is only fully understood when it is distanced from statistics and made personal. The news media call these "human interest" stories and relegate them to the final minutes of the evening news or the inside pages of the Sunday paper. I prefer to think of them as "human connection" stories. "Only connect," E.M. Forster wrote, and so we must. There is a section of the Holocaust Museum designed specifically for children. One of its rooms holds a bulletin board filled with index cards on which the young visitors have used pictures and words to reflect on their experience. I will never forget the card of an eleven-year-old Cherokee boy. "This made me sad. Because my people had something sad too, it was called the Trail of Tears." Under his words he had drawn a cluster of weeping stick figures. His people? Mine? It made no difference; weeping together, witnessing together, we were all connected.

To achieve that connection, women who have survived domestic abuse must tell their stories again and again, and we must hear more and more, until they…and we…find the meaning within them. I offer this collection of stories to help us discover that meaning.

About the Women

The stories in this book are true. They are not case studies, nor are they composite sketches. Since I began teaching and writing about domestic violence in 1994, hundreds of women have generously shared portions of their stories with me. Their memories bubbled up and spilled over. In part this was because they recognized in me a fellow survivor — someone who would understand. Mostly it was because I listened with compassion and without judgment. I never asked, "Why didn't you..." I never admonished, "You should have..." I said, in fact, very little. I conducted in-depth interviews with thirty women, and ultimately selected twelve to include in this book. The interviews, which lasted anywhere from 45 minutes to three hours, were taped and later transcribed. Working from the tapes, the transcriptions, and my own notes, I have rendered a faithful portrait of each woman. I present them to you as they presented themselves to me.

My goal has been to capture what is unique about each woman's voice; consequently, all quotes are accurate, only occasionally edited for clarity. The facts of each woman's life are also accurate. I have, however, changed such identifying details as names and places. Many of these women are still at risk from their abusers. All are entitled to their privacy.

Their willingness to be interviewed should not be taken lightly. You dig around like this, and memories come wiggling out like worms. Each woman who entrusted me with her story had stomped the earth down strong and tight. But the worms were still down there, alive and thriving under the hard-packed surface. Talking with me was the first time that many of these women had allowed themselves to revisit their history, to re-live their feelings of shame, pain, betrayal, and fear.

It is awful to listen to these stories. But we must listen. I have written this book because I want others to see these women as I see them. They are neither submissive martyrs nor comic-book heroines. They are real people who faced dif-ficult situations, had limited options, and made tough choices.

It has become fashionable to transform victims into plucky survivors, as if to imply that there is always light after dark-ness, that personal tragedy always leads unerringly to rebirth. The truth is that no life has such clear delineations. These women all survived domestic violence, yet they are much more than simply domestic violence survivors. These are ordinary people, leading ordinary lives. At the same time, they are ex-traordinary human beings. I do not glorify battered women. I do not hold them up as braver, stronger, or more courageous than everyone else. But they nonetheless deserve to be hon-ored for their bravery, their strength, and their courage.

Acknowledgements

I am indebted to the many members of the medical profession who confirmed that this book was important. They include Drs. Janice Asher, Peter Goodwin, Jody Heymann, Christine Peterson, Steve Ratcliffe, and Tom Schwenk. Special appreciation goes to Dr. Michael Magill and Dr. Leigh Neumayer at the University of Utah School of Medicine, for generously providing the "bookends" for this work.

Thanks to Greta DeJong at *Catalyst* Magazine for publishing the essay that started it all. Thanks to Judith Kitchen, Dr. Rachel Naomi Remen, and Leslie Stern for telling me that I am a writer. Thanks to Joan Michel at *Hadassah* Magazine, and to my friends at Jewish Women International and the National Council of Jewish Women, for helping me get the word out to the Jewish community.

Thanks to the women who graciously shared their stories and to the hundreds who have written to say that my words helped them heal.

Thanks especially to my dear friends who listened: Nettie Bagley, Ann Clark, Wendy Erekson, Julie Jonassen, Dede Lewis, Susan Makov, Rose McKay, Nicole Mertes, Kat Roman, Jane Schwenk, Eileen Stone, and Linda Vigor.

Finally, my heartfelt thanks go to my family. To my father, profoundly missed, who was always proud of me. To my mother, my role model, with deepest appreciation for her support. To my husband, Neal Whitman, who has been at my side throughout. This book would not exist without his unqualified enthusiasm, conviction, and belief in me.

Section I
Why Don't They Just Leave?

"You mean to say he beat you up? I never would have put up with that crap from my husband. Why didn't you leave?" Many people have trouble understanding why a woman stays with an abuser. They project themselves into the abused woman's place and visualize themselves walking away at the first sign of trouble.

But leaving is never the simple act it may appear to be at first glance. Each woman whose story appears in this section had her own reasons for staying. Yet despite the humiliation, fear, and isolation she endured, each ultimately managed to escape from her abuser. These are stories, not of frailty, but of clarity, resourcefulness, and strength.

1
My Story

Why It Took Me 8 Years, 7 Months, and 21 Days

*My story did not end on the day I left. I thought it had.
I told myself I had put the whole sorry mess
behind me; I gloried in my social and professional
triumphs. Though I knew my successes were real and
deserved, another part of me was tilting against the
windmill of my ex-husband's abuse; a windmill that had
long since stopped spinning.*

If, in 1965, you had been asked to vote for Girl Most Likely to Marry an Abuser, you would never have voted for me. I would never have voted for myself. Jewish. A doctor's daughter. Editor of the high school's poetry magazine. College-bound. Not what you'd call popular, but always a cluster of like-minded girlfriends and a boyfriend or two. The boyfriends were generally bookish and short. Some (though I liked to think not all) of my appeal lay in the fact that I was equally bookish and shorter. I was, in the parlance of the 1950s, "a well-brought-up young lady."

My parents worried about the sorts of things that all parents of daughters in Westchester County, New York, worried about in those days. Homework. Cigarettes. Interfaith dating. Premarital sex. They tended to hover a bit. But one fear never crossed their minds: the possibility that I would marry an abusive man. Throughout high school and college I dated boys who wore glasses, played either chess or cello, and wanted to save the world. I'm sure my parents worried that one of these boys might get me pregnant; they never worried that he would beat me. Yet in 1967 that was precisely what happened — within a week of my marriage to my college sweetheart, a man I will call Melvin Kesselman. Eight years, seven months, and twenty-one days later, I left.

I have spent more than twenty years trying to unravel the threads of physical and psychological violence that made up the fabric of that marriage. Why bother? Why not just be grateful that I got out safely? Because I still have nightmares, sometimes. Because, although the musical *Carousel* is quite beautiful, I can't watch Billy Bigelow slap Julie Jordan's face…and hear her sing sweetly that when someone you love hits you, it really doesn't hurt. Because when I watch the movie *Gaslight*, where Charles Boyer deliberately and methodically drives Ingrid Bergman to madness, I cry…and I remember. And because after O.J. Simpson's arrest, during the brief spasm of media interest in domestic violence, I overheard a woman in the beauty parlor smugly proclaim, "You know, I have no patience for women like Nicole. Why don't these women just leave? She should have walked out the minute he raised a hand to her."

She should have. The glib answer to women in abusive relationships. Common wisdom used to be: "Well, if he beat her up, she must have done something to deserve it." These days everyone is more sophisticated; no one would ever say a woman deserves to be abused. But the blame is still there: "She should have called a therapist." "She should have called her mother." "She should have called the police." "She should have been more assertive." "She should have been more accommodating." "She should have just walked out." When people hear that a woman is being abused, they say *she should* — never *he should.* They say, "Why doesn't she just leave?" not "Why doesn't he just stop?"

I know it's not as simple as that. I've read all the research. I know that batterers are themselves in pain. I know that they abuse, not out of anger, but out of a desperate need to control. I know they can't just stop; that they need professional help. And I sympathize, just as I sympathize with drug addicts. I'm no longer angry with Melvin (though this took me years to accomplish). But I am angry — hotly, fiercely angry — when I hear, "Why don't these women just leave?" To me, this question is as meaningless as asking the victim of a train wreck, "Why didn't you just drive to work that morning?" Nevertheless, I am going to tell you why I didn't leave; or, rather, why I spent so many years trying to make the marriage work.

I didn't leave…because abuse wasn't supposed to happen to women like me. I was married in 1967; the term "domestic violence" didn't exist. No one thought to join these two words, since no one accepted that domestic violence happened. A man would have to be a large, hairy, semiliterate alcoholic to be a wife beater, we all imagined — assuming that anyone ever gave the matter any thought. Domestic violence happened to women married to men who put away a few six-packs every Saturday night, got into a fight behind the roadhouse, came home roaring drunk, and threw furniture around the house. Domestic violence certainly didn't happen to nice middle-class girls from the suburbs. These girls went to college, married nice boys, taught school for a few years, started a family, and joined the PTA. This is what my girlfriends and I were raised to believe. This is how I thought the world worked. So when the abuse started, on my honeymoon, I had absolutely no way to frame what was going on.

I didn't leave...because I thought it was my fault. My only experience of marriage was the years I had spent growing up in my parent's home, where I saw warmth, kindness, and love. If my marriage looked nothing like theirs, I assumed that I must have been doing something wrong. And, of course, that's what Melvin kept telling me. He would become angry for no reason that I could see, and throw me against a wall — then say it was my fault because I had "egged him on." Lying in bed that night I would replay the incident over and over in my mind, trying to pinpoint the exact moment where I had gone wrong. I always found it, too. "I guess when he told me dinner was disgusting, I shouldn't have cried; I should have just laughed it off." "I guess I should have just ignored him when he called me a fat dummy, too useless to live." "I guess I shouldn't have gotten so upset when he announced that he wanted to have affairs with other women, and that if I didn't like it, I was uptight and possessive."

I didn't leave...because I believed I could fix it. During our two-year courtship Melvin was tender and affectionate. He told me I was the most wonderful girl in the world. (In the 1960s we were all "girls." So were our mothers. And our grandmothers.) After we married, he told me that I had changed — that I was no longer the cute, bright girl he had married — and I assumed he must be right. Rational people don't suddenly turn violent for no reason, so I must be giving him a reason. I clung to the image of the man Melvin had been before our marriage. I thought that if I could just get it right he would love me again.

I didn't leave...because after a while I began to believe what Melvin kept telling me: that I was overreacting. Yes, I would tell myself, he punched me in the stomach, threw me on the ground, or choked me...but at least he never gave me a black eye or a broken arm. Yes, he would delight in pointing out an obese woman on the street and saying "See her ass? Yours is even bigger."...but perhaps I did need to lose weight. (I weighed 107 pounds.) Yes, he would indicate another woman, tall, blond, and voluptuous, and scold, "See her? Why can't you look like that?"...but this was the late 1960s, when the Beach Boys wished we all could be California Girls, so maybe a petite brunette couldn't hope to be seen as attractive. Yes, he would occasionally put a pillow over my face while I slept, watching with detached interest as I woke up gasping for breath...but the next morning he always acted as if nothing had happened, so I had to be imagining it, didn't I?

I didn't leave...because there was nowhere to go for support. There was no place I could tell my story and be told "It's not you — it's him. There's no way you can 'get it right' because he needs you to get it wrong." I never confided in a rabbi. I had been raised to believe, still believed, that Jewish men are not wife-beaters, that my husband was the sole exception. Why would a rabbi believe me? I barely believed it myself. I never confided in my internist. I had no obvious injuries: my eyes were not blackened, my ribs were not broken, my jaw was not shattered. Without such dramatic evidence, why would a doctor believe me? I did convince Melvin that we needed marriage counseling, and the two of us began weekly sessions with a psychiatrist. There, I struggled to find the right words to pin down his actions: "If he goes through a door ahead of me, he gives it an extra push to let it swing back and hit me." "He sneaks into the bathroom when I'm taking a shower and turns on the cold water tap in the sink to make the shower scalding hot." "Every day feels like a walk across a mine field." The psychiatrist insisted that I was morally obligated to stay in the marriage because my husband couldn't function without me. He also lectured me about my own contribution to what he termed "your marital fights": I had to stop being my father's Little Girl and become my husband's Adult Wife, become the sort of woman Melvin would want to treat well. Since this advice came from a physician, I assumed it must be correct. Melvin and I spent two years — one hundred hours — with this man. Then he pronounced me "cured," reminding me that everything would be just fine if I put my energy into supporting my husband. So I tried even harder to be the perfect wife.

I didn't leave...because I grew accustomed to living a lie. He never pushed, tripped, or slapped me in public. He was generally careful to frame his taunts and gibes so they appeared to be nothing more than innocuous teasing. Thus, to our friends, Elaine and Melvin Kesselman were the perfect couple. Melvin called this Not Airing Our Dirty Linen, and I agreed. Of course I agreed. I was to blame for his abuse, and I couldn't manage to figure out how to be the sort of wife he cherished. Which, he promised, he surely would — if I could just learn how to make him happy. A wife who can't make her husband happy: why would I want that to become public knowledge? I agreed to the charade and I played my part well. Which probably explains why, when I finally did leave, he got to keep the friends; no one understood why I'd want to leave such a charming man.

I didn't leave...and then one day I left. Why? It sounds so trivial in retrospect, but such turning points often are. Melvin and I had recently moved to Manhattan. He had graduated from law school and taken a job with a prestigious corporate law firm. After five years as an elementary school teacher, I had started graduate school at Columbia University. One spring afternoon, we stood on a street corner at a downtown crosswalk. I looked up and saw a particularly lovely old pre-war building with a magnificent garden on its terraced roof. I pointed and said, "Isn't that building beautiful?" "Which one," sneered my husband, "you mean the one over there that looks exactly like every other building on the street?" A woman standing beside us wheeled abruptly and said, the way only a New Yorker could: "She's right, you know. That building *is* beautiful — and *you* are a horse's ass." The light changed and she strode off. Such a tiny incident: she probably forgot it by the time she reached the other side of the street. Melvin and I eyed each other, but neither of us said a word; to all outward appearances, the woman might never have spoken. And yet, I felt something shift inside me. For the first time in eight years someone had confirmed the belief I had once held but long since relinquished: it wasn't me. It was him. The following winter, I announced that I was leaving.

Yes, of course it took more than a single turning point. Breaking free of abuse is always a process. My professors at Columbia told me that I was a talented instructional designer and encouraged me to enter the doctoral program. Fellow students became close friends. Many of them had never met Melvin — I was more than half a couple. With professional and personal success, I stopped caring about, hardly noticed, my husband's abuse. I told him the marriage was over on December 25, 1975: the day I turned twenty-seven. He cried and begged me to stay. He told me how much he needed me.

He said he couldn't imagine life without me. He swore he would change. I barely heard him.

And so I left. I am one of the lucky ones. He didn't try to stop me. He didn't threaten me. He didn't stalk me. He didn't murder me. Some men do. I am one of the lucky ones. The impact on the rest of my life has been minimal. I didn't become homeless. I didn't turn to alcohol or drugs. I didn't enter into a series of abusive relationships. I didn't commit suicide. Some women do. Instead, I went on to earn a doctorate and develop a successful consulting practice. I published two books. I married a gentle, compassionate, altogether extraordinary man. Together we have built a strong and loving marriage.

Life is good. But my story did not end on the day I left. I thought it had. I told myself I had put the whole sorry mess behind me; I gloried in my social and professional triumphs. Though I knew my successes were real and deserved, another part of me was tilting against the windmill of my ex-husband's abuse; a windmill that had long since stopped spinning. Each man who found me attractive, each business client who praised my expertise, each friend who treasured my presence, were incontrovertible proof that Melvin had been wrong.

I did sometimes wonder why it was so important to prove him wrong. After all, the woman on the Manhattan street corner had summed it up pretty well: he was a horse's ass. So why did his opinion matter? It was years before I finally understood. During the eight years, seven months and twenty-one days of this abusive marriage, I never once realized that I was an abused woman. I knew Melvin hurt me. But I never understood that every one of his actions was part of a carefully orchestrated campaign to hurt me. I knew that he sneered, criticized, heckled, yelled, shoved, tripped, choked, bit, and slapped. When I attempted to defend myself he ridiculed my protests, accusing me of being insecure, possessive, neurotic, psychotic. He would rage: "You're sick, Elaine. You're twisted. You're warped." I didn't believe him. How could I? And yet I did believe him. How could I not? He shaped his insults with surgical precision, knowing precisely which words would make me doubt my own perceptions. Some domestic abuse experts write of the "cycle of violence," drawing diagrams of perfect rectangles and circles, models of clarity and precision, to illustrate this pattern of abuse. But I never saw a pattern, because I never knew I should be looking for one.

Patterns of any sort are often hard to spot. There is an artist whose canvas is the tilled soil; living plants comprise the colors in his palette. In several acres of Iowa farmland he once planted the *Mona Lisa*. Visitors who wandered through the tended beds saw nothing but flowers, leaves, stems, and bark; the famous woman with the elusive smile could only be seen from an airplane. The pattern of my husband's abuse was equally difficult to grasp. As a result, when I eventually found the strength to leave, I didn't quite understand what I was leaving. I didn't truly understand that I was safe. I thought I had to keep protecting myself, to ensure that this would never happen to me again. And so I drew a magic circle, stepped carefully inside it, and relied on its protection. Like the child who wishes on the first star, like the baseball player who steps to home plate, spits twice, and runs his index finger along the brim of his cap, I created my own set of rituals to keep myself from harm. Melvin had a beard; I dated only clean-shaven men. Melvin was a fussy and finicky eater; I looked for men who cared little about food. Melvin spent long hours studying car and stereo magazines; one attraction of the man who later became my husband was his lack of interest in all things mechanical. When I married Melvin Kesselman, I eagerly embraced my new monogram. When I married Neal Whitman, I kept my maiden name.

I believed that my magic had worked because my new husband never abused me. It was years before I realized that Neal never abused me, not because of anything I was or wasn't doing, but because he isn't an abuser.

It was many years before I finally saw the pattern of my first marriage, before I named what had happened to me, before I understood that I had been a battered wife. Once I did, I was able to step outside the magic circle.

Nearly all my wounds have healed. The scars are barely visible. But I still have flashbacks, especially when the evening news blares the horror of one more woman beaten or murdered by a man who told her he loved her. I still have nightmares, especially when I teach or write about domestic abuse. Yet the process of gathering and giving voice to the stories in this book, which sometimes triggers nightmares, has also launched new dreams.

I call one of these The Phantom Apartment. In this recurrent dream, I am standing in a tiny studio apartment. As I look about me, I am aware that I moved here recently, that I live alone, and that I have just left Melvin. It is a five-story walk-up in an old building, so small that there is barely room for a single bed and a two-burner stove. Three tall windows face onto a dark alley. The size and general dreariness of this apartment would ordinarily depress me: I prefer large sunny rooms. Yet in my dream, I am wildly happy. I am free.

✿ Reflection ✿

Melvin and I dated for two years before we married. Why hadn't I spotted his abusiveness? For years the question itched like a vague indeterminable rash. I should have known. I should have realized. I should have spotted him as a threat. What signs had I missed? Take the matter of his nicknames. His mother still called him by his baby name of "Mellie." His high school friends, unable to resist the bait, dubbed him "Smellie." Was this a clue to his personality that I had been too stupid to catch? Well, of course not. Many kids saddle their friends with annoying nicknames. My dearest girlfriends called me "Shrimpy." That's what kids do. Still, like a compulsive archaeologist, I laboriously sifted through the dust of our courtship until, bored and irritated with what felt like an obsession, I would berate myself for wallowing. The marriage had ended years ago. I was safe, for heaven's sake. Why couldn't I let go?

Sometimes, in the middle of a perfectly normal day, I would find myself experiencing a flashback. Several years ago, hiking in California with my husband, I tripped over an exposed root. Not unusual: although I am generally graceful, at odd, unpredictable moments I turn into a klutz. As Neal reached out to steady me, my mind lurched through time and space. Could this memory be real? Being subtly pushed or knocked off balance by Melvin, never for any particular reason, unable to predict his next sneak attack. My body eventually learning to trip on its own, instinctively picking the time and place to minimize risk of injury. In Harvard Square I stumble on a bit of broken pavement. "Dummy," Melvin snorts, smiling slightly, rolling his eyes at my clumsiness. I giggle nervously. Embarrassed, unhurt, safe for the moment.

Sometimes these flashbacks would transport me to the first apartment I shared with Melvin. I wasn't simply remembering the apartment; I was actually there. Everything was in place: the furniture, the wallpaper, even the quality of light. And Melvin. Melvin would also appear, unbidden, unwanted, in my dreams. He still does.

Good values, necessary for the healthy functioning of a family, get twisted in an abusive relationship. Consider the value of loyalty. "Don't tell the other kids at school that your little brother wets the bed," we tell a nine-year-old. "In our family, we stick up for one another." I was raised with a firm sense of family loyalty. In the post-war era of the 1950s, loyalty in suburban America meant that husbands supported the family financially while wives supported their husbands by keeping the home fires burning under a pot of chicken noodle soup. My father developed serious heart problems when I was sixteen. His deep love for my mother, and hers for him, were never more clear to me than during the weeks she spent beside his hospital bed. Their loyalty to me was equally strong, wrapping me in a snug quilt of assured security. Home, quipped Mark Twain, is the place where, when you go there, they have to let you in. For me, home was the place where I knew I was loved.

So when the marriage counselor insisted that Melvin couldn't function without me, I was betrayed as much by my own sense of loyalty as by the therapist's ineptitude. Suppose Melvin had developed diabetes? Suppose a random car collision had left him a paraplegic? I certainly wouldn't have left him under those circumstances, any more than my mother would have left my father after his first heart attack. I had married Melvin for richer, for poorer, for better, for worse. Well, it was definitely worse, and wasn't likely to get much better. Didn't that mean I had an obligation to stay?

My sense of loyalty kept me in my marriage; so did my sense of isolation. Most of Melvin's abuse took place in secret, away from witnesses. The woman on the street corner in New York City was, to the best of my memory, the first person to validate my feelings. To the best of my memory...memory being, I acknowledge, unreliable. It may be that others gave me similar messages. It may be that the woman on the street corner offered the message at precisely the time I was ready to receive it. I often wonder what would have happened if the incident had occurred three years earlier. Or during my first year of marriage. I might have turned on her, a loyal wife fiercely defending her husband. "You've got a helluva nerve," I might have replied. And she would have walked away, mumbling to herself about moronic masochistic women.

In the midst of a lecture to a group of physicians, one of the participants challenges my statement about the strength of abused women. Not so, he insists. He has a patient whose boyfriend routinely beats her up. Each time she arrives at the clinic with fresh bruises, he launches into his prepared speech about her safety. Using all his powers of persuasion and his white-coat mantle of authority, he tells her she must leave this man. She refuses to listen. This physician is about ready, he tells me, to stop trying. I understand his feeling of frustration, I reply, but I believe his patient is listening, and that she will leave her abuser when she believes she can. I remember how I

clung to the words of the woman on the street corner. I re-
peated them daily, my private mantra.

He's a horse's ass.

He's a horse's ass.

You know what? He really IS a horse's ass!

So why on earth am I wasting my time with him?

2
Judy North

It Was As Though He Had an Invisible Whip

My mother said, "Judy, he has an invisible whip that he's just whipping you with all the time." I thought, you know, he has whipped me enough. I am not going to allow him to whip me any more.

A border of cardboard teddy bears frames the doorway. The letters of the alphabet march with military precision across the top of the chalkboard. A hamster sleeps in a corner of his wire cage, all but invisible under a heap of cedar shavings. Seeds sprout in paper cups along the sunny windowsill. Construction paper leaves, each bearing a wobbly first and last name, are taped to the windows. Judy and I sit crouched in chairs that were designed to accommodate rear ends considerably smaller than ours. The tops of my knees graze the bottom of my chin. When I was an elementary school teacher I sat this way all the time — but I was a lot younger then. Now that I've managed to sit down, I wonder if I will be able to get up again without a boost.

Judy North has had years of practice extricating herself from undersized furniture. She has been teaching first grade here in Fremont, Nebraska, for twenty-five years; long enough that a few of the six-year-olds in her current class are the children of the students she taught when she began her teaching career. Fremont is about 75 miles north of Omaha. Towns-people rarely make the drive. Judy's great-great-grandparents were among the group of Scandinavian farmers who made their way here in the middle of the nineteenth century and built the town. One of her great-uncles is a Lutheran minister. Her mother's father was the mayor of Fremont. Her grandmother lived to be ninety-seven. As Judy describes her childhood, I can't help being reminded of some of the sturdier characters in Willa Cather's novels. "My mom and dad were very hard workers and instilled in us the idea that you work hard and you get a good education. I did not see my dad being mean to my mom or my mom being mean to my dad. So when all this happened to me, I just didn't know what to think. I was really taken aback."

Not only had Judy never seen cruelty at home, she had never seen it anywhere. Judy was a late bloomer; her social life took off once she started college and continued during the first few years of her teaching career. At the time she met Karl Millhauser, she was dating three other fellows. "But Karl was the only guy I'd ever been in love with, and so we married." First comes love, little girls chant, their feet dancing nimbly over the spinning jump rope, then comes marriage. Judy North became Judy Millhauser. It seemed ideal. She and Karl were both in their mid–twenties. They were both public school teachers. Their work schedules were identical. They had sum-mers off. The school system had generous maternity leave benefits; they could begin a family right away. Within a year of their marriage, Judy gave birth to Cyndi. Four years later, Breanna was born. And two years after that came Matt.

While his wife was busy having babies and teaching first grade, Karl was working diligently to drive a wedge between

Judy and her parents. "He'd criticize things they did. And he'd be sure to pick things that bothered me about them, too. So then I'd think, well, yeah, he's right. And I'd start to be mad at them." She feels dreadful now when she remembers how coldly she treated her parents. At the time, of course, she didn't realize that the tensions between them were being engineered. She had no way of knowing, for example, that when Cyndi was born, Karl did not call her parents to tell them they had a granddaughter. And Judy's parents had no way of knowing that this deliberate neglect took place without her knowledge or consent. It was two days before Mrs. North came to visit Judy in the hospital. By the time she arrived, mother and daughter were furious with each other. Each felt betrayed. How could my daughter have a baby and not tell me? How could my mother show so little interest in her new grandchild? It dawned on neither of them that the betrayal was Karl's.

A grandchild generally brings families together. In Judy's case, the opposite was true. "There were times when I would see my Mom pull up in front of the house, but I wouldn't open the door. I could just cry now, at the hurt I caused her. I've had a hard time forgiving myself for that. After about five years I did start to let her in sometimes, and Karl would find out and say, 'Your mom's been here, hasn't she?' I'd find myself lying to cover up. And then I'd have to live with that." Although the ties between Judy and her parents were tenuous, she never doubted their love and support. On their part, as they watched the thin veneer of Karl's good manners peel away, they began to realize what sort of man their daughter had married. They were not shy about telling her so. Once, in the heat of an argument, Karl took a swing at Judy's father. Her brother and cousin, witnesses to the attack, got out of their car and stood shoulder to shoulder beside Mr. North. No words were spoken; none were needed.

After that episode, Judy's father made it clear: if Karl were ever to raise a hand to her, she should call the police. But Karl never did raise a hand to her. His abuse was a slippery thing, hard to catch hold of. "My mother always said he was trying to drive me crazy. It took me a long time to see it. It was, like, if I can get her to go nuts, then I've succeeded." The more she reflected on her mother's insight, the more she realized the truth of it. "We come from good, strong, pioneer stock," her mother reminded her. "Stand up to him."

The night she did was the night she ended up in the emergency room. On the previous afternoon, the family had gathered to celebrate Matt's first birthday party. There were balloons, crepe paper streamers, and a chocolate cake topped by a parade of dinosaurs circling a single candle. Judy's older brother held the camera, ready to capture the moment when his nephew either blew out the candle or put a chubby arm into the cake. Suddenly the front door flew open. In came Karl. He muscled his way past the group, went upstairs to the bedroom, and locked the door. There was an instant of shocked silence, followed by a determined babble of conversation as everyone tried to pretend that nothing out of the ordinary had happened. The candle was vanquished, the picture was taken, the song was sung, and the cake was eaten. But Judy was mortified. How could Karl have humiliated her in front of everybody?

Early the next morning Judy stood in the school's front office, running off some papers on the mimeograph machine. One of her colleagues asked how the birthday party had gone. And Judy burst into tears. "Up until that time, nobody knew.

At least, I thought no one knew, but it turned out that they all did." It isn't easy to keep secrets in an elementary school — especially when it's the only elementary school in a town the size of Fremont. The other teachers had often witnessed Karl bringing Judy to work, yelling insults out the car window at her hunched back as she scurried into the building. They had had their suspicions, but discreetly said nothing. "And, see, I thought I was hiding it really well, but I wasn't. It was like I was living in another world." Now the worlds had collided.

Once Judy started to cry, she couldn't seem to stop. "My principal saw what was happening. He got me into his office so that parents, teachers, and kids wouldn't see what was going on. When I got in there I just totally lost it." The principal could see that Judy was in no shape to teach that day. How did she feel, he asked, about talking to a professional about what was bothering her? Judy could only blow her nose and nod. She was too wrought up to drive. Her mother picked her up, drove her to the therapist's office, and sat in the waiting room while Judy poured out her story of the hundreds of belittling, deliberate cruelties that had punctuated her nine-year marriage. The therapist listened carefully. Then he delivered his verdict. The next time Karl treated her badly, she was to fight back. "Grab him by the arm," he suggested. "Grab him by the arm, pull him around to face you, and say 'If you call me a shithead any more, I'll let the air out of your tires.'" Judy could barely believe what she was hearing. How could letting the air out of Karl's tires help her marriage? Besides, what if Karl were to hit her? Then, the therapist calmly replied, she should call the sheriff.

The incompetence, the sheer *badness* of the therapist's advice rocks me back in my chair. I can't even begin to imagine what he could have been thinking. Did he believe that Karl's abuse was caused by Judy's lack of assertiveness? Suppose she had reported that she often stood up to Karl, matching him insult for insult, shout for shout. Would he then have advised her to duck her head and meekly accept her husband's behavior? Judy recalls the rest of the session. "We spent about an hour in his office, rehearsing what I'd say to Karl. He had me shouting, and screaming, and even hitting a pillow. And I thought, well, he's the professional, so maybe this will work." That afternoon Judy marched confidently back to her house determined to follow the therapist's advice. She invited her mother to stay for dinner — an invitation she had not risked since she was a new bride. Why *couldn't* she invite her own mother to a meal? How *dare* Karl stand between them? She slammed pots and pans down on the stove, taking pleasure in the satisfactory clatter. She was a new person! She wasn't going to let Karl push her around ever again! Just let him try!

An hour later, he did. "I was fixing dinner and he started in arguing with me, calling me names. I turned and I just yelled, right in his face, 'If you ever call me dumb fuck, or a shithead, or a fat pig, ever again, here's what I'm gonna do to you.'" The next bit is a blank. Her mother has told her what happened, but Judy has never recovered her memory. Head trauma will do that. She gropes for words, summoning her recollections in disjointed fragments. Karl, drawing back his fist. The jolt of pain as his knuckles connected with her jaw. Though she has been told, she doesn't remember that the blow was hard enough to send her flying across the room. She doesn't remember that her head hit a corner of the windowsill, knocking her out cold. She doesn't remember her children screaming, certain that their mother was dead.

The paramedics came. The sheriff came. But by that time, Karl had simply walked out of the house, gotten into his car, and driven away. An ambulance brought Judy to the hospital. She had suffered a concussion. Her jaw was dislocated. She was in a neck brace for weeks. But the pressing question that night was where she should go next. Her family didn't want her to go home. What if Karl came back? They also didn't want her to go to a shelter. Strong pioneer families like the Norths don't send their daughters to battered women's shelters. Those shelters are for other sorts of women. And so they brought Judy and their three grandchildren to their house, where they remained until Judy was well enough to go back to work.

Another conversation that night concerned Karl. Mr. North asked the sheriff if criminal charges should be filed. Wasn't the attack on his daughter a clear-cut case of assault and battery? Well, yes, said the sheriff reluctantly, but if Judy were his daughter, he wouldn't be all that eager to press charges. Karl could lose his job. Which meant that Judy and the children would lose a breadwinner. "The sheriff told me to just let it go and file for a protective order, so that's what I did. I look back now and I think, yeah, I should have filed charges. I mean, he did commit a criminal act. But my biggest fear was not so much him losing his job. The fact that scared me, that convinced me not to file charges, was that if I caused him to be arrested, would he come after me? So I didn't do it."

After Judy's injuries had healed, she and the children moved back home. Karl, of course, was living elsewhere; the protective order that Judy had filed the day after his attack prevented him from making any contact with the family. Judy flushes as she tells me the next part of the story: the part where she allowed him to move back into the house. "This is something my parents don't completely understand. Why would I do something like that? I don't really understand it myself, other than thinking…well, you know, maybe we should give this one more try." I understand. Judy took her marriage vows seriously. She and Karl had made three babies together. And now he was apologizing, saying it would never happen again, and agreeing to therapy. I imagine the conversations she must have had with herself. Maybe this incident has finally shown him how serious this is. Maybe he's gotten a good scare. Maybe our marriage can be saved after all.

They began seeing a marriage counselor. "You don't call names," the counselor scolded them both, setting down rules like a soccer referee. "You don't hit. You don't yell." Rules for the two of them…as though they were equal partners. Within a few weeks, Judy could see that she had made a dreadful mistake. Karl didn't want to make their marriage work; he wanted to make her pay for her defiance. The abuse started again, each act more bizarre than the last. He threw her students' homework papers into a snow bank. He smeared peanut butter in her hair. Driving home from one of their therapy sessions, he reached across her to the passenger door, released the latch, and tried to push her out of the car. The vehicle careened across the road at freeway speed; had she not been wearing a seat belt, she could have been killed. Nevertheless, this was not the turning point for Judy. The turning point came several days later, triggered by an incident that seemed comparatively mild. "It was ironic because the first physical assault happened February 9th, and on April 9th he punched me in the arm. It was like he was a lot smarter, punching me in the arm instead of the face." With every punch, Karl made a threat.

He would take Judy's checkbook and write a bunch of bad checks. Punch. He would burn her clothes. Punch. He would sell her car. Punch. Finally, he accused her of having an affair with the principal of her school. "He said, 'Look at you, getting all dressed up for him.' My kids were just standing there watching this. And all at once I realized I had had enough. I took off out the front door, went to the next door neighbor's house, and called the sheriff. I filed for spouse abuse. I went through it for sure that time. I was done with him."

Statistics indicate that, on average, battered women return to their batterers five times before they leave for good. Judy beat those odds. But even after it was over, it wasn't over. Neighbors reported that they would occasionally see Karl driving slowly up and down the street. Bills and letters sometimes mysteriously went astray. Judy tried to avoid being anywhere that she and Karl might run into each other. She used to shop in a supermarket near the junior high school where he taught science, but she found a new place to buy her groceries. After she turned a corner in the Omaha convention center and ran smack into Karl, she stopped attending the annual Nebraska Education Association conference. Now and then his car would pass hers on the freeway. Was it a coincidence, or was he following her? Karl's stalking — if that's what it was — was as subtle as his abuse had been. She could never prove that he was the person breathing into the other end of the phone at two o'clock in the morning or sneaking away from school during his lunch hour to rifle through her mailbox. It was, she thought, as though Karl wanted to keep her from ever feeling completely safe and relaxed.

There are women who, at this point, would have bought a handgun. I can sympathize with the fear behind such a purchase, but I cannot condone it; weapons of violence can, and too frequently do, provoke more violence. Judy found other ways to undercut Karl's power. The first was to reclaim her maiden name. "I had so much negative emotion associated with his name. Judy Millhauser...ugh! Taking back my name just kind of made me feel like I was obliterating this marriage." Perhaps from her years of dealing with rooms full of six-year-olds, Judy is extremely literal-minded. The day her divorce was final, the day she was legally entitled to use her maiden name again, she armed herself with the thickest, blackest magic marker she could find. It has always been Judy's habit to write her name on the title page of her books. With the precision of a military censor, she located every book in the house that she had purchased since her marriage. Back and forth went the marker over her married name. "Every once in a while I'll come across a book that has Judy Millhauser in it, and I still take that marker and just cover it over. Then I turn the page to look at the back." If the letters are still visible on the reverse side of the page, she smears a layer of ink there as well, completely eradicating every trace of her former name, her former life.

I can just see Judy striding purposefully through her house, brandishing the ideal weapon of choice for a first-grade teacher: a magic marker. She also found a creative use for the whistle that hung around her neck during recess, its sharp call a signal for her students to form a neat line at the base of the school steps. "I knew it was him calling me. He tried to muffle his voice, but my daughter and I both recognized his laugh. I mean, who else would call me up all hours of the night? So I brought home my playground whistle from school, and I blew into the phone. I just blew it as loud as I could, and I thought, hey, that's too bad if I blast your eardrum. You shouldn't be doing this to me."

The phone calls stopped. Instead, Karl found another way to keep Judy off balance. First, he took her to court in an attempt to get custody of the children. Not that he particularly relished fatherhood; during his visitation weekends, he often failed to show up. But a custody battle was, he knew, an excellent way to frighten his ex-wife. After he lost, he began to withhold child support payments. Judy never knew when his check would arrive. For the past two years he has sent no money at all. She spent an enormous amount of time, energy, and attorney's fees trying to work through the court system, trying to force him to pay what he owed. Recently, though, she has decided to stop fighting. Her income is sufficient to support the family. And she is tired of dancing to Karl's tune. "My mother said, 'Judy, he has an invisible whip that he's just whipping you with all the time.' I thought, you know, he has whipped me enough. I am not going to allow him to whip me anymore."

Judy has been single for eleven years. When she was newly divorced, she dated a good many men, believing that she had an obligation to provide a replacement father for her children. But nothing ever came of these relationships. One reason, she concedes, is that she held back, unsure of her ability to pick a man. Suppose another abusive man were to appear in her life. Would she be able to spot him? "Karl treated me nicely when we were dating. He sent me flowers, you know, and he really sweet-talked me. And then he was just a different person when we got married. So it made me question myself, question if I ever truly was in love with him. Maybe it was just infatuation. I wonder if I even know what love is? I mean, I would hope that now I would know. But could I ever be sure?" These days, Judy goes out on fewer dates. She is less concerned that her children are growing up without a father. Cyndi graduated from high school last year and has been accepted to nursing school. Breanna is actively involved in her high school drama club. Matt is an enthusiastic soccer player. "I haven't found the right person that will fit into our family," she tells me. "We're gonna be really picky. The kids and I figure that if I find someone, then good, but if I don't, that's good too. It would be nice to be married. But I don't want to rush into anything. I've met some real nice guys. But I've also met some real jerks!"

As our interview draws to a close I shift a bit in the tiny chair, trying surreptitiously to restore the circulation to my knees before I attempt to hoist myself into a standing position. Does she realize, I ask her, how strong a person she is? "I do," she replies. "I just keep building and growing and getting more independent. Yes, I think I'm strong. At first I didn't think so. I'd been put down and my self-esteem was shot. It took me a while to get it boosted up again. And even now, he'll do something to get at me, and I can feel it slipping down. But, you know, I'm at the point where, if I let him know that it's bothering me, then he wins. It's that invisible whip. Now I just think, well, big deal. I won't lower myself to his level."

"In fact," she concludes, a mischievous glint in her eye, "I had an uncle…bless his heart, he's since passed away…who used to say that Karl was lower than whale shit at the bottom of the ocean. And that's pretty low."

❧ Reflection ❧

Why didn't Judy leave Karl sooner? I believe one reason was that she didn't realize that he was an abuser. Difficult, yes. Nasty. "He sure has a mean streak," she would say to herself when a sharp insult or a cruel sneer would leave her close to tears. But she never thought to label herself a victim of domestic violence. Judy is not unusual — I hear stories like hers all the time. "I almost wish he had hit me," a woman writes in an e-mail. This is not masochism. It is easier to have clarity about your circumstances when you can look in the mirror and see a black eye. Harder by far to pin down the cruel insults or oblique threats, the words melting away even as you attempt to examine them.

Even physical violence is not always straightforward. My friend Ellen describes her ex-husband's attacks as "sneaky." His abuse was a covert operation that kept her constantly off balance and unable to quite pin down what was happening. Once he watched as she stood in front of the stove stirring a pot of soup; when the liquid began to boil, he walked casually behind her, bumping her with his elbow. She fell against the red-hot pot, nearly capsizing the liquid. She shows me the inch–long scar where her hand touched the pot. Ellen considers herself lucky: if the pot had overturned, she would have had burns all over her body. She shakes her head as if to clear away the vision of that kitchen. "The worst part was afterwards, when I accused him of pushing me deliberately. He shook his head in mock pity and told me that I had quite an imagination. Not only had he not pushed me — he hadn't even been in the kitchen. I felt like I was going mad."

An abused woman's family can see it. Her friends can see it. Sometimes her co-workers can see it. So why can't she see it? Because it is astonishingly difficult to see what cannot be comprehended. "I'll believe it when I see it," the old expression goes, yet in fact the opposite is true. We see it when we believe it. It took me many years to name my marriage as abusive. I knew Melvin's words and actions made me miserable. What I couldn't believe — never imagined — is that he coldly and deliberately said those particular words, took those particular actions, precisely for that reason: to make me miserable. During their courtship, Karl showered Judy with flowers, gifts, and loving attention. Judy didn't realize that he was an abuser for the simple reason that he didn't act abusive. Once they were married, though, the relationship began to change; the changes so subtle that she could never pinpoint when they began or how they escalated.

Abuse is not a slap, a punch, or a curse. Abuse is a campaign. A vigorous concerted effort to accomplish a purpose. A process of deliberate intimidation intended to coerce the victim to do the will of the victimizer. Like a military campaign, Karl's abuse was mounted with patience and precision. To better understand such a campaign, it helps to compare an abusive relationship with a non-abusive one. Karen likes scrambled eggs with onions and cheese. Onions give George, her husband, heartburn. So early in their marriage they reached a reasonable solution: Karen prepares sautéed onions in a separate pan, scrambles a skilletful of eggs, and tosses the onions on her portion before bringing the plates to the table. Karen is happy, George's tummy is happy, and they get on with their day. Perhaps you're thinking "Well, of course. That's just what we do in my house, only it's liver. Or broccoli." Lucky you. Your relationship isn't abusive.

Leah isn't so fortunate. She prefers her Saturday morning breakfast eggs with ketchup. Her boyfriend, Stuart, loathes the very thought of ketchup on eggs. In a non-abusive relationship, this wouldn't present a problem. Ketchup is even easier than fried onions: one person pours the stuff out of the bottle, while the other doesn't. But Stuart is an abuser, and he is mounting a campaign. If Leah puts ketchup on her eggs, Stuart glares, snatches his plate from the table, and marches indignantly into the living room where he finishes his breakfast hunched in a corner of the sofa. Then he refuses to speak to Leah for the rest of the morning.

After a few weekends like this, Leah confronts Stuart. She's furious. "They're my eggs, dammit, not yours. Nobody's forcing you to eat ketchup. Since when is it your business what I eat?" Stuart doesn't hit Leah. He doesn't raise his voice. He simply looks at her sadly, slowly shaking his head from side to side. "Oh, Leah. You're twisting everything around. I'm not telling you what to eat. It's just that I can't smell anything except eggs, bread, and coffee in the morning. It makes me nauseous. I wish I could eat with you — I really do. But surely I shouldn't have to suffer nausea. It's such a pity that you won't support me in this one little way." Now Leah is confused. Stuart sounds so reasonable. Leah has always thought of herself as supportive; is she being selfish? After all, if Stuart is truly nauseous, his behavior makes some sense. She certainly doesn't want to make him suffer. Ketchup on eggs isn't that important. She can learn to do without it.

More than thirty years after the first summer of my marriage, I can see the start of Melvin's campaign, see the battles I lost in a war I didn't even realize was being waged. All I knew at the time was that I always felt tired, muddled, and slightly off balance. I lost my focus. I couldn't seem to concentrate.

My world had shrunk down to fit inside that one-bedroom student apartment. Like me, it never dawned on Judy that her marriage was abusive, that she was the victim of a campaign. In fact, she never thought of herself as a victim at all. Victims were women in emergency rooms with black eyes, broken ribs, or knife wounds. Then she became one of them. And within three months, she filed for divorce.

It would be a mistake to view the blow that sent Judy to the emergency room as Karl's single act of domestic violence. Possibly it was the one covert act that could not be ignored. For years, though, he had been practicing acts of sabotage: covert subterfuges designed to undermine Judy's credibility. He began with her family. From there, he moved to her workplace. Judy had enjoyed good relationships with the other teachers at school before her marriage. But Karl began to put doubts in her mind. They were out to get her, he warned ominously. She was so naïve — always thinking the best of people. Couldn't she see that she was working much harder than the rest of her team members? Judy pondered his words. Now that he mentioned it, she did seem to be doing more than her fair share at school. Narrow-eyed, she peered with suspicion at the women with whom she had happily shared closet space, lunch duty, and construction paper. Karl was right! They weren't her friends, after all! They had been taking advantage of her all these years, and she had been too trusting to realize it. As she withdrew from them, they responded in kind. Soon, without quite understanding how it had happened, Judy was as isolated at work as she was at home. "They don't like me," she thought to herself. "I guess they never did."

After her divorce, Judy learned that Karl's acts of sabotage had extended even further. With carefully manufactured hints, headshakes, and slips of the tongue, Karl had managed to convince their neighbors that Judy was hooked on tranquilizers and painkillers. They never confronted her, of course. It wasn't their place. But if Judy had ever come to them with claims of domestic violence, who would have believed her? "She's a real nut case," her neighbors would have whispered among themselves. "Not quite right in the head. It's all those pills she takes. Sad, really. Her poor husband."

Even assuming she believes the unbelievable, that her husband is deliberately telling lies about her, there is no way a woman can defend herself from this sort of sabotage. I return, as I will throughout this book, to my story. While Melvin attended law school, our apartment was the bottom floor of a two-family home in an old section of Boston. Miss Marie Donnelly, Radcliffe Class of 1925, was our landlady and upstairs neighbor. She was a lovely white-haired woman, the youngest daughter of a lace-curtain Irish family who had taught high school chemistry for forty years while dutifully remaining at home to care for her aging parents. A "maiden lady," she called herself, with, I think, a certain amount of pride. Her parents long dead, herself long retired, she supplemented her teacher's pension by renting out the first floor of the house where she had grown up and grown old. Miss Donnelly, I called her — never Marie. In her presence, I didn't feel like a third-grade teacher. I felt like a third-grader. The ceilings of the old house were thick, but not thick enough to stifle the sounds that spilled out of our apartment. Miss Donnelly must have heard the shouts, the accusations, the curses, the tears. She must have. Yet she never said a word.

The year after he graduated from law school, Melvin and I lived in a pretty garden apartment complex in Chapel Hill, North Carolina. One morning Metta Nesbitt, the pleasant, middle-aged social worker who lived in the apartment next door, came to call. I was puzzled by her visit; we barely knew each other. Nevertheless, I invited her in and politely offered her a drink. "Let's not," she sighed. Let's not? Let's not what? A drink, to me, meant a glass of ginger ale or a cup of coffee. We sat and chatted for a while. Drinkless. I never did learn the reason for Metta's visit. Her social work training must have led her to my door, a compassionate caseworker making a surprise home visit. Snooping, some might say uncharitably, but I prefer to believe that she was worried about us. About me. Like Miss Donnelly, though, she never referred to what she must have overheard through the thin walls that divided our apartments.

Two years later, on the day I announce I am leaving him, Melvin, in an orgy of self-loathing, confesses. He had told each woman that I was an alcoholic. He is a worm, he passionately declares. An imbecile. He only hopes I can find it in my heart to forgive him. (Despite his groveling, he will repeat the tactic several weeks later, sitting in my parents' kitchen, attempting to convince them to talk some sense into their errant daughter. "Elaine goes out drinking every night with her graduate school buddies," he whines earnestly. "She comes home drunk. I'm worried about her." My parents, bless them, are having none of it. "*If* that's true," my mother says, leveling him with a look of clear-eyed severity, "and I don't *for one moment* believe that it is, then you must be making her terribly unhappy. Which tells me that she needs to be as far away from you as possible." A few weeks later, Melvin's mother tries a more oblique approach. "Isn't Elaine being silly!" she sighs, inviting my mother to commiserate over their shared troubles. "No," replies my mother calmly, "as a matter of fact, I don't believe she is being in the *least* bit silly." And that was that.)

Melvin's empty accusations would have been laughable, if they weren't so pathetic. Of all the rumors he could have spread, this was probably the most far-fetched: from the day I turned eighteen, the legal drinking age in New York State, until I reached my late twenties, I had consumed a total of perhaps a dozen drinks. My idea of a cocktail had never progressed beyond the syrupy sweetness of a Tom Collins, the favored drink of college girls in the 1960s. But that refined elderly spinster, that concerned social worker, had both believed him. Of course. Why would a man say such a thing about his wife unless it were true?

3
Mandy Winchester

I Kept Trying to Get It Right

Part of me was saying, I'm not foolish to be afraid, I'm not paranoid, I'm not being neurotic...this is wrong. And the other part of me was believing what Adam was saying: that it was my fault. That if I would just fix things, it would all be fine."

Judy North spent nine years defending herself from a campaign she never knew was being waged. Mandy Winchester spent more than twice that in a futile effort to please a man who would not be pleased. "I must be doing something to provoke him," abused women tell themselves. "No one behaves this way without a reason. If I can just figure out how to get it right, he'll be nice to me."

Mandy met Adam Winchester precisely where she had expected to meet her future husband: at college. "I was an English major, and seriously wanted to be a writer. But at the University of Virginia, we used to say we were in school to earn our M.R.S. degree," she laughs ruefully. "Can you believe it?" Indeed I can. My friends and I said the same thing at Boston University. A college girl's program of action, though unwritten, was as clear as the distribution requirements set forth in the B.U. course catalogue. Freshman girls were supposed to spend the year doing reconnaissance among the available upperclassmen. A year was considered ample time to locate and land a man. The successful coed would be pinned during the second semester of her sophomore year, engaged over Christmas vacation in her junior year, and married the summer after graduation. Mandy was on a fast track: she was married on Valentine's Day of her senior year.

Adam was, everyone agreed, an excellent catch. He had graduated with honors from the University of Virginia and, at the time of their wedding, had completed his first year at Vanderbilt Law School. He was well on his way to a successful legal career. Adam Winchester, Attorney at Law. The title fit him as well as the custom-made suits and polished wing-tip shoes he wore each day as he made the hour-long drive from Bernardsville, New Jersey, to the Trinity Square financial district at the base of Manhattan.

Twenty-two years later, when Mandy finally decided she had had enough of both Adam and his clothes, he was quick to throw his success in her face. "You are never going to succeed in this world," he taunted. "Wait until you're out there single and you try to support yourself. When you try to fit into the world that I'm in, you'll see what a failure you are." Mandy and I are approximately the same age; we both went off to college in the mid-1960s, our suitcases stuffed with matching skirt and sweater sets, blouses with Peter Pan collars, penny loafers, and knee socks. She never expected to have a career, never wanted to achieve Adam's sort of success. Her job was to maintain their home, raise their children, and give dinner parties. To be, in short, the perfect lawyer's wife. To be, in short, perfect.

This is not to say that every woman who chooses full-time motherhood over investment banking, neurosurgery, or corporate law will become the victim of domestic abuse. Those who marry abusers will. Those who don't, won't. Mandy did. And perfection became the yardstick by which her husband measured and controlled her. "I kept trying to get it right. Twenty-two years is a lot of years of not being able to trust your own inner voices — your own intuition. To me, that was a huge part of the damage that got done. Because part of me was saying, I'm not foolish to be afraid, I'm not paranoid, I'm not being neurotic...this is wrong. And the other part of me was believing what Adam was saying: that it was my fault. That if I would just fix things, it would all be fine."

Fix what sorts of things? Mandy honestly can't remember many details, and admits that the ones she can remember would not impress anyone who hadn't lived through them. Like the secret drip, drip of battery acid under the hood of a car, no single drop responsible for the inevitable destruction of the engine. "It wasn't any one dreadful thing, like a beating. It was just lots of little things. It felt like the rules kept changing." An outsider would have described the Winchesters as the ideal family. But, says Mandy, it was all a sham. Take the matter of their family vacations. "My parents thought we had the perfect marriage. They thought we had the best family because we went on all these trips. When I finally got divorced, I said to my mother...Did you know that I planned every trip? I would do all of the household things, I would pack all the bags, I would make all the arrangements. Then I would pack the car, load the kids, drive to wherever we were going, and Adam would show up like a houseguest. At the end of the trip, he'd make an excuse and leave early and I would pack everything up and drive the kids back and unpack the car. That's how we had a perfect family. Because I did it."

Mandy studied Adam as a naturalist might study the habits of a particularly ferocious species of snake, trying to predict where he would strike next. She would arrive home at the end of the day and pull her car into the driveway. She would push the remote control, the garage door would slowly open, and she would watch — her pulse racing — to see if Adam's car was in the garage. "As the door would lift, inch by inch, I would keep my eyes fixed on the place where his tires would appear. Because if they were there then I knew he'd be home. And I'd be afraid…because I never knew who he would be." A seasoned hiker will walk confidently past a well-fed rattlesnake basking on a sunny rock, certain that the snake will not suddenly rear back and attack. For twenty-two years, Mandy never once felt this degree of certainty. It didn't matter if she and Adam had spent a wonderful night and chatted pleasantly over breakfast. Later that day, for no reason Mandy could see, Adam was equally likely to arrive home in a good mood or in a rage.

"Usually it would happen when he was in pain over something. He'd go to the office and sit and ruminate. He'd stew and stew until he had worked himself up into a rage, until the point where he was furious with me. Then he'd come home out of the blue, in the middle of the day, and unload on me until he'd get me emotionally overwrought. It was like I could see him walking through the door with a huge bag of shit. He would keep handing it to me, and I would keep rejecting it, until finally I couldn't push it away any more — I was burdened by the shit. Then I'd be crying, he'd be feeling great, and he'd leave and drive back to the office. And when he came home again that night, he'd be fine. Because he had dumped all his shit on me."

Adam would be happy, he assured her, if only she were a better wife to him. Better in what way? If she truly loved him, he insisted, she would instinctively know. Mandy stops for a long minute, hesitating, unsure how much she is willing to reveal. Finally she takes a deep breath and continues. There was one significant part of their marriage, she admits, that she never, ever managed to get right. Sex. I can see that it is not easy for Mandy to discuss these intimate and embarrassing details. Her face is pinched tight; her words come out in little bursts. Adam, she says, insisted that they have sex every day. For a moment, I don't understand what she is telling me. Then I consider the implications behind this seemingly innocuous statement. Every day. Even if she was tired. Even if she had been up all night with a sick child. Even if she had a headache...or menstrual cramps. It simply wasn't an option for her to refuse. "And even then, I could never seem to satisfy him. It was never kinky enough, it was never erotic enough, it was never different enough, it was always too traditional."

Mandy's voice takes on an angry edge as she remembers how incompetent Adam made her feel in bed. "I mean, he's got what he's got, he puts it into what I've got, in and out, and that's sex, folks, right?" I suppose so: stripped of the love and intimacy that one hopes would accompany sex between husband and wife, that certainly captures the basic mechanics of the act. There are, after all, only just so many possible combinations and permutations. "Oh, but not for Adam," she snorts. "Let's do it in the whirlpool at the health club. Let's do it in the hallway of the hotel. Let's do it on the side of the highway in the back seat of the station wagon. Oh, it was just madness. Nothing sexual was ever good enough. I was doing exotic make-up. Pearls. Push-up bras that cut my flesh. Wigs. Trying to look like Dolly Parton. We'd have whips and chains and hooks and ladders and I'd fall asleep exhausted, thinking, well finally he's satisfied, and the next morning he'd be furious with me. Because it hadn't been good enough."

It strikes me that Adam's sexual demands were not really about sex at all. Sex was part of Adam's campaign to ensure that Mandy would devote every minute of her existence, every ounce of her energy, to meeting his needs. Truly, there was no significant difference between the black lace push-up bra and the Beef Wellington-Potato Soufflé-Poached Asparagus-Baked Alaska dinner that Adam expected to see on the dining room table whenever Mandy entertained his business associates. Whether it was her Dolly Parton costume or the perfectly rolled collar of Adam's starched white Sea Island cotton shirt, Mandy's life was centered on the impossible feat of getting it right. And Adam was the one who defined right and wrong.

It also strikes me that it would have been impossible for Mandy to explain to those around her that she was a victim of abuse — assuming, that is, that she even realized it herself. Adam expected her to entertain his clients with fancy dinner parties...but was that really so unreasonable? Adam was fussy about his clothes...but weren't many Wall Street lawyers focused on fashion? "He wants sex every day," she once hesitantly confided to a girlfriend. "Lucky you!" was the response. "My husband and I used to make love all the time when we were first married, but now he's only interested about once a month." How could Mandy have made her friend see that Adam's sort of sex had nothing to do with making love — that it was not about love at all, but about control? As long as Mandy was constantly dreaming up new ways to please Adam in bed, she couldn't be reading her favorite books, playing her favorite music, developing her writing skills, even — especially — noticing how much of her energy went toward keeping Adam happy.

Adam's sexual demands would reach fever pitch when-ever her attention was momentarily diverted away from him. Narcissism, she calls it in retrospect, though at the time she never knew there was a name for what Adam did, never knew she was its victim. One weekend Mandy and Adam met friends in Vail, Colorado, for a weeklong ski trip. The three couples rented a three-bedroom condo with a large open common area that contained living room, dining room, and spacious gour-met kitchen; the plan was to ski all day, make dinner together, and spend the evening visiting. As Adam and Mandy unpacked in their bedroom, Adam announced that the two of them would sneak away from dinner early that night. "He said that we could take a sauna together, then do all this wild lovemaking out-side in the snow, and then go into the bedroom and keep going all night. And I said, 'Well, of course' — because I knew that's what I was supposed to say, that it was what I'd better say." But after dinner, their friends suggested a Scrabble tournament. "Oh, I love scrabble!" enthused Mandy. "I haven't played since college. What a great idea!" The five friends played for hours, while Adam seethed angrily behind a copy of the *Wall Street Journal*. By the time they were finally alone in the bedroom it was after eleven o'clock…and Adam was furious. Mandy had sold him out. She had promised him sex after dinner, and then deliberately involved herself in a stupid board game. Mandy tried to explain that she had simply forgotten, but it was no use. "He was in an utter rage. The vacation was ruined and it was all my fault. He spent the rest of the week pouting and sulking — he was hateful. I spent my time trying to de-cide how I could get enough pharmaceuticals to kill myself."

It would be another six years before Mandy left Adam.

But that vacation marked a turning point in their marriage. Were it not for her four children, Mandy believes that she might well have committed suicide. "But I didn't want to leave them with that legacy. I just couldn't do it." Instead, she started allowing herself to see her marriage as it really was, peeking behind the façade that she had carefully built over the years, the façade that everyone, including Mandy, believed was the truth. She held imaginary conversations with Adam. "I started thinking about it. I thought, I want an adult relationship: an equal, adult relationship. I don't want to be your mother; I don't want you to be a little boy who can indulge your whims. It's not appropriate that you spend your money however you want and I have to make do out of the grocery money. And that you make all the big money decisions and I don't have a part in that." The pattern, Mandy began to realize, had been set early in their marriage. "First he was trying to get good grades in law school, so that he would make law review. Then he was building his law practice. I told myself that it was for our future, that it was about us. But now years had gone by, he had everything, and I had nothing. It was never going to be about us. It never had been." The light went on. It was always going to be about Adam.

Life paths are never as linear as they appear in retrospect. Looking back at her marriage, Mandy recognizes the Vail fiasco as the start of a series of small changes that, over the next six years, transformed her into the woman who agreed to meet me today. She signed up for a creative writing workshop. She joined a book discussion group. She occasionally met female friends for lunch; if lunch turned into an afternoon of conversation, she didn't always rush home in a panic to cook Adam's dinner. "What turned me around was just starting to believe that I deserved something better in my life. For instance, I had always had crooked teeth. They were not terribly crooked, but they were crooked. Well, my kids were all having orthodonture, and the orthodontist said, 'Why don't we do you, too?' And I said, 'Let's do it.' It was a small but significant step. From there I started taking more small, but significant steps until eventually I was able to tell Adam, 'Here's what I need in the marriage.' Of course, that didn't happen, because he wasn't about to change. And at that point the marriage was over."

Divorcing a successful lawyer is never trivial. Adam offered a financial settlement that represented, at most, ten percent of his net worth, threatening a lengthy and costly legal battle if she didn't accept his offer. "He said, we can do a settlement or we can litigate. And if we litigate, I've got legal resources. It won't cost me anything, and your attorney will end up with all the equity in the house, it'll drag out for years. So, I did a very strong thing. To some people it might not look strong, but believe me, it was. I took his offer and I left. It takes power away from people like Adam when you don't fight with them. I knew if I'd fought with him on his turf, I would have continued to be the victim of what he was doing to me."

They put the house on the market; while they were waiting for it to sell, Mandy moved into an apartment. After all the years in a large house, I ask, did a two-bedroom apartment feel like a demotion? She smiles at the memory. "I was as happy as a clam. I adored it. I had a little stereo system, I put my own music on...I was exquisitely happy. I got strong and did a lot of the healing while I was still married to Adam. So when I got divorced, I was soaring. I was healthy and strong and vibrant and happy. When they heard we were splitting up, people would say, 'I'm so sorry.' And it was very misplaced sympathy. I mean, where were they six years ago when I was suffering? I'm not suffering anymore."

❧ Reflection ❧

You may be asking yourself why Mandy tolerated Adam's emotional and sexual abuse for twenty-two years. You may believe that, had you been in her shoes, you would have left immediately. For many years after I divorced Melvin, I berated myself for not having ended the marriage earlier. What psychological flaw, I wondered, caused me to stick with this abusive man for over eight years? But when I reflect on Mandy's story (and — inevitably — reflect on my own), it strikes me that part of the answer can be found in the concept of cause and effect.

Children learn this concept early in life. I was in kindergarten. I came home crying that Sharon hit me. I can still hear the singsong of my mother's reply: "Do you mean to tell me that Sharon marched up to you, out of the clear blue sky, and hit you?" I hung my head and sheepishly confessed. "I told her she was a doody head. Then she stuck her tongue out. Then I pulled her hair. *Then* she hit me." My mother has a special way of raising her left eyebrow that is guaranteed to strike terror in the hearts of grown men and small girls. Up went the eyebrow...and I shriveled. I had just learned a useful lesson. My actions had consequences; if I didn't like the consequences, I'd better change my actions. Children hear this lesson for what feels like an eternity. "You got a B on your spelling test? Better study harder next week." "You want to be in the marching band? You'll have to spend more time practicing that clarinet." "You want to race for the track team? I'd lay off those cheese quarter-pounders, son." Under normal circumstances, cause and effect — though aggravating to those on the receiving end — works. Children grow into adults with the self-discipline to achieve their goals, and eventually teach the same lesson to their children. But in the fog of an abusive relationship, especially a relationship like Mandy and Adam Winchester's, where abuse took the form of psychological control and sexual coercion, cause and effect becomes a trap.

Imagine it. You met a nice guy. You fell in love. You dated for a year. Three weeks ago you got married. Tonight you decide to make meatloaf for dinner. You're an enthusiastic new bride, so you take a bit of time with the familiar old recipe. You add a little garlic powder, mix in a few breadcrumbs for texture, and even remember to peek into the oven once to make sure the meatloaf isn't turning into a dried-out brick. An hour later when your husband arrives home from work he brushes past you without a word. Slightly puzzled, you consider asking him if anything is wrong, but decide to cut him a little slack. He's probably just tired. Besides, it's his apartment, too — he's entitled to be antisocial now and then. He sits down at the table and you fill two plates with meatloaf, baked potato, and green beans. He looks down at his plate, then looks up at you. He takes a bite of the meatloaf, chewing with his head cocked to one side, rolling the food in his mouth for a prolonged minute. Then he smiles — an odd, twisted smile, quite unlike any expression you have ever seen. He stands. He picks up the plate of food and ceremoniously carries it to the sink, where he scrapes the contents into the garbage disposal. "This meatloaf tastes like shit," he explains calmly. "Do you honestly expect me to eat shit??" He leaves the kitchen and walks into the living room, settles comfortably on the sofa, and aims the remote at the TV set.

You stand in the kitchen, stunned. Do you say to yourself "Yikes! I married an abuser! I've got to leave him immediately!"? Do you pack your bags and walk out of the apartment, the marriage, the new life? Of course not. Mandy didn't, I didn't, and neither would you. You think, "I must have done something to make him act this way. He wouldn't be upset at me for no reason." Cause and effect. Then you think about meatloaf. In fact, you think about meatloaf for quite a while. Maybe garlic powder wasn't such a good idea. Freshly crushed garlic has a better flavor. And you used stale bread for the breadcrumbs; maybe you should have used fresh bread and toasted it. You were late getting home from work. Much as you hate to admit it, you were operating on autopilot. You feel slightly ashamed of yourself. That sort of cooking was acceptable when you were single, but you're a married woman now. The next night you again prepare meatloaf. You spend an extra half-hour chopping garlic, toasting fresh bread, and correcting the seasonings as the meatloaf cooks. And your husband is delighted with the dinner! So you say to yourself, "Now I know how to make him happy. I just have to pay careful attention when I cook his meals."

The next time, though, it isn't meatloaf; it's the length of your dress. It's too short. He screams that you look like a slut. You're confused: didn't he love that dress when you were dating? You start to wear your dresses longer. He sneers that he never realized he had married such a frump. You find yourself standing in front of the mirror for long minutes, trying to guess the ideal dress length.

The time after that, it's the streak you left on the windshield when you washed the car. Or the fifteen minutes you spent on the phone with your sister. Or the TV shows you like to watch. Or the TV shows you don't like to watch. Until, little by little, everything you do is directed at one goal: to act in a way that will keep this man from hurting you. You believe that your behavior caused his anger. That all you have to do is "get it right" and you'll have a good marriage. This is how cause and effect — the good lesson you (and I, and Mandy) learned as a child — becomes a trap in an abusive relationship.

Because there is no way you will ever get it right.

Because he needs you to get it wrong.

Mandy spent twenty-two years trying to get it right. I spent eight. Would I have divorced Melvin sooner if I had not learned the lesson of cause and effect so early and so well? It is an interesting question. The lesson that kept me in an abusive marriage was the same lesson that helped me graduate from college, teach school, earn a doctorate, and build a consulting practice. In retrospect, it is a lesson I am glad my parents taught me. I would not have had them do otherwise.

Mandy told me her story in the living room of the small house she purchased with the proceeds of her divorce settlement. While an interview with Mandy had not been the only goal of this trip, it certainly had been one factor in my decision to travel 2,000 miles to the East Coast. The other was an opportunity to reach a group that is just beginning to take action against domestic abuse: the previous day, I had delivered the keynote address at a seminar for religious leaders.

The event was a success, earning praise from the participants and a brief clip on the evening news. I was to have been part of that clip. When the seminar ended I was ushered into a narrow little room where a technician tinkered with lights and a reporter peppered me with questions. Fortunately, the television producers chose not to use any of this footage. Silly me: I had expected his interview questions to be about domestic violence. I was ready with facts, figures, and powerful stories of the impressive women I have met in my travels. Caught completely off guard when the reporter asked me why I didn't leave Melvin, I found myself spouting a babble of inane justifications. My words came haltingly, thick and stupid, as I attempted to encapsulate eight complicated years into a sixty-second sound bite.

Live and learn. My best comebacks always happen at least twenty-four hours after the fact. As I left Mandy's house and drove along leafy suburban streets to the airport, I replayed the scene in that cramped little room. I saw myself turn cool eyes toward the reporter. I heard myself reply, in Mandy's voice as well as my own, "But, you see, I *did* leave."

It is impossible to work in this field without encountering The Question. Why doesn't an abused woman simply walk away from the man who is abusing her? What's her problem? Why doesn't she just leave? When I was just starting out, I naïvely and enthusiastically tackled the answer. I talked about isolation, insecurity, fear, housing, the judicial system, childcare, and poverty. I quoted the statistics: a woman is at greatest risk during the six months after she leaves an abuser than at any other time in the relationship. I rambled on and on, my justifications sounding, even to my own ears, like excuses. No matter how I shaped my answer, the inquisitor's response never varied. Yes, the man or woman would smugly reply, but surely she could have done *something*. On a scale of one to ten for stubbornness, I rate a twelve. Once again, I would take a deep breath, patiently explaining how difficult and dangerous it is for a woman to escape from an abusive man. And once again, my answer would fall flat, my audience unmoved, unconvinced.

Eventually, it dawned on me that the people who ask the question are not waiting for an answer. They are making a judgment. The question, which is not a question at all, suggests that a battered woman's life is entirely in her own hands — that her abuser's actions are her problem, her responsibility. That what is significant is not the abuse itself, but her response to it. As though, after a bank holdup, we were to ignore the man with the stocking mask and semi-automatic, examining instead the bank teller, theorizing about her childhood, her family, her self-esteem. It is a trivializing question, a weary dismissal. It implies that the problem is not domestic violence at all. The problem is the women who refuse to take action.

I no longer frame my answer around The Question. Because the simple truth is that battered women do leave. They leave all the time. Against all odds, often at enormous risk, they leave. Section II, "Getting Out," tells the stories of three abused women who broke free.

Section II
Getting Out

Just as there are many reasons why a woman stays with an abuser, there are also many reasons why she eventually leaves. The stories in this section illustrate that getting out of an abusive relationship is always a complex process.

Every battered woman goes about extricating herself in a different way. For some, it is a series of gradual insights leading to the inevitable conclusion that leaving is the only viable option. For others, the decision to leave is triggered by one dramatic incident. In all cases, the decision to leave is a courageous one. Because no woman ever simply "leaves" an abuser. She escapes. Leaving is what you do when the movie is over.

4
Peg McBride

I Assembled the Jigsaw Puzzle

To me it was like pieces of a puzzle. You know, one
puzzle piece doesn't make a whole lot of sense.
In fact, maybe it says nothing.So although his abuse was
progressive, what also was progressive
inside of me was those puzzle pieces. Once I got enough
of them to see his face for what it really was,
I think maybe that's when I could leave.

Peg McBride was twenty years old when she and Ira Klein stood before a Justice of the Peace at the Denver Courthouse. "That should have been a tip-off for me," she says with a wry shake of her head. "He's not springing for a big wedding." They had met three years earlier, when Peg was a college freshman and Ira was a senior. A bit uncertain of her own intellectual ability, Peg looked up to Ira. She admired his talent, his creativity, and his sophistication. Ira made documentary films. He had spent his junior year studying in Italy and France. He spoke three languages. Every horizontal surface in his small apartment overflowed with books. Peg was from a large, exuberant family. In the years when Ira and his older brother sedately toured European museums with their parents, the six McBride children fished, skied, skated, and played noisy games in the backyard of their suburban house.

Peg's first date with Ira set the pattern for their relationship, a pattern so faint as to be virtually invisible. Ira wanted to see a performance of "Waiting for Godot." Peg was hoping to catch a showing of the just-released film, "All the President's Men." Ira politely agreed to Peg's choice, and off they went to the movie. He never let her forget it. Months later, he would manage to weave her faux pas into the fabric of their conversations...particularly when those conversations took place in front of an appreciative audience of Ira's friends. What a child she had been, picking Robert Redford over Samuel Beckett! He could see that she had a lot to learn. He could see that he was going to have to teach her the difference between True Culture and mass market schlock.

Over the next three years, Ira was always delighted to instruct Peg, but — though she would have been hard-pressed to explain why — his lessons left her feeling more unsure of herself than ever. "In the three years we were dating, he never actually came right out and called me stupid. But he knew that's what I was most afraid of, that I really was stupid, that everyone else knew more than me."

"Stupid" is probably the last adjective I would consider applying to Peg. She is a remarkable poet. She is also a forklift operator who, three years ago, decided to "climb down off her horse" and write full time. Peg describes her journey from factory to poetry as she and I and twelve other men and women sit around a conference table in the Yarrow Hotel in Park City, Utah. Today is the first day of a weeklong writing workshop, part of the annual Park City Writers at Work conference. Sometimes, good things happen at this conference. Friendships form. Scraps of ideas assemble themselves into full-fledged manuscripts. Unknown writers get discovered. This is my first year here; my first experience, in fact, with any sort of writing workshop. Earlier in the day, as I prepared to make the forty-five minute drive over the mountain range that separates Salt Lake City from Park City, I felt like a twelve-year-old poised nervously on the brink of junior high school. I was awake hours before I needed to leave the house. I agonized over outfits. I spent an extra twenty minutes styling my ordinarily wash-and-wear hair. I even contemplated eyeshadow. What would all the other girls in the workshop do? Was it better to stand out with too much makeup, or disappear with too little?

By the end of the week I hadn't been discovered — no book agent handed me a sterling silver tray piled high with a million-dollar book contract, international movie rights, and a fat cash advance — and I had abandoned the eyeshadow. But I had received plenty of good advice and a gratifying amount of praise. And I had met Peg. With her own experience of abuse tucked safely into a corner of her past, Peg didn't know if she had much of a story to tell. There were no guns, no arrests, no dramatic courtroom scenes. Ira had been out of her life for years. But he occasionally popped up in her poetry.

Loose Love

Eh why you bein so m(e)an to me? I haven't done a thing.
Because you can.

Pushed me up against a door
Because you can.

Drew your fist
Because you can.

Broke your fist on my head
Because you can (produce irony).

All this name callin', because you can,
Has got to stop this moment,
Because I can
Go walking
out the door. ("Because you can," will leave you lonely.)

You know what?
I can, I can,
love without a fist. Love without any power over what I love.
I can love loose.

Because you can('t) keep me, you cry.
You must cry for yourself.
'Cause you never cried for me.

Because you can't.

Peg and I talk about the insidiousness of abuse — drops of water on stone, collectively forming a channel that splits the stone in two. Her poet's vision examines, then ultimately rejects this obvious metaphor in favor of one that rings vividly true to us both. A manufacturing metaphor. Suppose, Peg muses, you have a length of straight pipe that must be bent into an elbow. Superman heroics aside, such a pipe cannot be bent all at once; the dense, noncompliant metal would simply buckle. The trick, she explains, is to put tiny little bends into it. Working slowly and deliberately, each incremental adjustment builds on the one before it, until the pipe conforms to the new shape.

This is how Ira's abuse appears to Peg now. A series of tiny little bends, each rather trivial, each easy to ignore. "There was a progression with it. For the first year, it wasn't very present. There were just a couple of remarks that were like zingers. Ouch!...you know, but I kind of got used to it as his personality. And then the second year we were dating, I thought...God, the guy can be pretty tough, but I love him, and there's so many good things about him that I'm gonna stick with it." Because Ira never hurt Peg physically during their courtship, she did not recognize his nasty remarks or cruel jokes as the deliberate campaign of psychological abuse that she sees so clearly in retrospect. "I thought, hey, it's not the biggest part of our relationship; there's so much good to it too. So let's say the first year it was ten percent. And then the next year it was twenty percent, and the next year it was thirty…"

Which still left seventy percent that was really good. On the basis of that seventy percent, Peg married Ira. And that's when Ira's abuse turned physical. The first time he hit her, she blamed herself for the attack. "I had been drinking at the time, and I was sure that if I hadn't been drinking and sort of acting out or mouthing off, that he would have never touched me." In a way, finding a rational explanation for Ira's abuse was comforting to Peg. She couldn't control Ira, but she could certainly control herself. If her drinking had caused his attack, the solution was obvious: no more drinks. The next time Ira hit her, though, she hadn't been drinking. As far as she could tell, she hadn't been doing much of anything. "I felt like it was without pattern. I tried to find a pattern to it; in fact, I spent a lot of my days thinking about a pattern so I could get this pattern set out in front of me. I figured if I found that pattern, then certainly I could avoid it. But the guy was so patternless with the abuse that I couldn't defend myself. I didn't know how to overcome it. I didn't know how to get away from it."

Peg considers herself lucky: Ira's physical abuse was never violent enough to cause her severe injury. One push sent her flying across the room, the white of her eye suddenly red from the web of blood vessels broken when her face hit the edge of a table. Generally, though, her injuries did not show. His favored technique — chosen, perhaps, because it did not leave visible marks — was to pound the top of her head with his fist. (Once, in a faintly delicious bit of irony, the blow was hard enough to fracture Ira's hand.) Peg never felt that she was in serious danger from Ira. Twenty-two years later, though, she still winces as she recalls the vicious words he used as whips. With exquisite precision, Ira directed his taunts at Peg's deepest insecurity. "He really sensed that I was afraid of being stupid. It was my weak spot. So he tried to drive that one home. 'You're so stupid…you don't know *that*? I can't believe you don't know that. You're just…I can't *believe* you're that stupid. I just can't *believe* it.' Da, da, da…on and on and on."

It would be a mistake to visualize Peg and Ira's marriage as nothing more that an endless series of insults punctuated by a few well-placed punches. For one thing, Ira worked long hours in his studio. His film projects took him on location to South America, Africa, and Europe. For another, their daughter, Rachel, was growing into an active toddler who kept Peg busy with the ordinary routines of motherhood. Weeks would go by without incident. Meanwhile, the pattern she had searched for so assiduously in the early days of their marriage was beginning to emerge. "To me it was like pieces of a puzzle. You know, one puzzle piece doesn't make a whole lot of sense. In fact, maybe it says nothing. So although his abuse was progressive, what also was progressive inside of me was those puzzle pieces. Once I got enough of them to see his face for what it really was, I think maybe that's when I could leave."

As Peg collected the puzzle pieces, she began to see that Ira's abuse was a strategy on his part — a strategy designed to keep her attention focused on her flaws and away from his. "One day I was thinking about it and I thought, you know what? We have this thing going on where we talk about all these negative things about me, but I never get to critique him. I mean, it just never happens. We don't talk about his mistakes. About how he's a little bit overweight. Or that he maybe isn't the smartest person in the world either. We never get to that. So I started to do it silently. Every time I saw a new piece of the puzzle, I'd put it away in the drawer. I didn't announce that I was starting to form a picture of who he was. I kept it to myself. I'd say to myself: 'Okay, Ira, let's take a look at you now.' I did it quietly… I knew instinctively that was the only way."

Eventually, Peg had accumulated enough pieces of the puzzle to compose a distinct picture of Ira's face. Warts and all. Then, when she was eight months pregnant with their second child, an argument started. She doesn't remember what the argument was about. It isn't important. What she does remember, quite clearly, is that he kicked her. He had never hurt her when she was pregnant with Rachel; this was something new. "He kicked me right in the ass. You know, when you're that pregnant, you've got a baby's head pressing down there pretty heavy duty. Something about that was like…I've gotta get the hell out of here pretty quick."

The puzzle pieces had resolved themselves into a true picture of her marriage; with that picture firmly in place, Peg was no longer willing to tolerate Ira's abuse. Nevertheless, she did not pack her bags that day. She was, after all, eight months pregnant. She had a two-year-old. She did not have a job. Where would they live? How would they eat? She could have gone to her parents for help, but hated to burden them with a situation as alien to them as it was to her. Peg had rarely seen her parents argue. She had certainly never seen punches, kicks, or deliberate cruelty in the McBride household. Ultimately, Peg decided that she wasn't in any immediate danger. She had time to consider her options.

A few weeks later, Beth, their second daughter, was born. The delivery was uneventful, but two days after Ira brought her home from the hospital Peg developed severe back pain and a high fever. She called her obstetrician and described her symptoms. He was concerned: it sounded to him as though she might have a kidney infection. She needed to get to the emergency room right away, he warned. If her kidneys shut down, she'd be in serious trouble. "So I got off the phone and I said to Ira, 'You know, I really need to go to the emergency room…I'm really sick.' And he said, 'No, I'm not gonna drive you. I've gotta get my sleep for work tomorrow.' So now I'm begging this guy, 'Please, you know, could I get to a hospital? I really, really need to go.' But he wouldn't take me. And so I'm laying awake there and thinking to myself…I could die here. And then all of a sudden it struck me. One of these days he's gonna kill me. He's gonna kill me in such a subtle way that nobody will know."

I can picture it. Poor Peg, her friends and family would say. She developed complications after her second pregnancy and she died. What a dreadful tragedy. Ira is beside himself, of course. But it's not his fault. It isn't anyone's fault. These things happen. Poor Peg.

Fortunately, Ira was persuaded to drive Peg to the hospital the following day, where she remained until her body managed to fight off the massive infection that had very nearly sent her into renal failure. In the hospital, away from Ira, Peg regrouped. And a week after Ira brought her home, she moved out. Peg's leaving was a quiet act. There were no dramatic announcements, no angry scenes, no fiery showdowns. "I was very low-key. I was still weak from the infection, and I had these two babies, so I called my parents in Fort Collins and asked if I could come to visit them for a while." Ira was perfectly willing for her to spend some time with her parents. He had to be out of town anyway: a script meeting in Dallas.

Except that Ira wasn't in Dallas, after all. He was in Bermuda. With his girlfriend. Peg had learned this interesting fact from her older brother, who played poker every Friday night with Ira's former college roommate. "He had told me he'd be back from Dallas on Saturday. He didn't call on Saturday, he didn't call on Sunday, so Sunday night I called him and I said, 'Hi, you didn't call me. I thought you'd give a call.' He goes, 'Well, I was really tired from Dallas…" And I said, 'Well, you know what? I heard that you were in Bermuda.' And he said, 'Yeah, I did go to Bermuda as a matter of fact.' At that point, I didn't get angry or anything, I just said, 'You know, I kind of think we should get a divorce.' And that was pretty much the end. I never went back."

It strikes me that Peg probably left Ira in the precise way necessary to guarantee her safety. She agrees. "It was perfect timing. He was getting very involved in a new film, he was doing a lot of cocaine, he was cheating on me, so all of that was almost like a distraction. He was distracted momentarily, and I zipped out the door. But I still did it quietly, you know. I saw him turn for just a minute, I saw him take his eyes off me, and I was outa there."

Within a month, Peg had found a job, moved into an apartment, and settled down to raise her two daughters alone. Ira urged her to come back, but he did not stand in her way. He did, however, stall her efforts to obtain a divorce. He was always ready with an excuse: he had to be out of town, he didn't have the money for a lawyer, he had no time to file the necessary documents. Unable to control Peg in any other way, the divorce became his final hold over her. "He couldn't have me, but he had that little piece of paper saying 'I own her.' Evidently he needed that." Peg saw Ira's tactics as no more than a minor nuisance; since she had no interest in marrying again, she simply let the matter slide. Once again, she sensed instinctively that she would be safest if she avoided direct confrontations with Ira. It wasn't until ten years later, when she fell in love with Phil, that Peg finally pinned Ira down long enough to get the divorce.

During the intervening years Peg had occasional dates, but never committed herself to a serious relationship. Though she wasn't a hardened cynic, she was certainly cautious about men. "When I was younger, I sort of lived in lollipop land. But after Ira, I wasn't naïve anymore. I saw something I couldn't see at the age of fifteen...or even twenty. There are some people that actually like hurting other people. I'm not someone who believes, if life hands you lemons, make lemonade. If you got shit, it is shit, you know, that's all there is to it...and abuse is real shit. But, on the other hand, I think my marriage taught me that there are people in this world who, for no other reason than maybe the pleasure of seeing someone in pain, will hurt you. Maybe that was a good thing to learn."

Peg met Phil Gleason when she was thirty-four. A high school teacher, he was easygoing, warm, and — fortunately — patient. Phil proposed to Peg a good many times before she agreed to marry him. He suggested that they combine the ceremony with a trip to New Orleans. They would fly to New Orleans, find a Justice of the Peace the following day, get married, and then spend a few days exploring the city. Peg chuckles as she remembers the trip. "Poor Phil. I really put him through it. We woke up in our hotel room and he was so excited to be getting married. And I said, 'You know what? I don't feel like getting married today. Maybe tomorrow.' The next day, I said 'I don't feel well. I'm a little nervous…let's just go out and enjoy the city.' The third day, I was, like, 'Uh, I've really got some ironing to do….' By now the poor guy's practically crying, and saying 'Don't you want to marry me?' Finally, on the fourth day, I realized I just had to get ahold of myself, and we got married. He was so sweet about the whole thing. I really appreciated that."

Peg and Phil have been married for ten years. But it took the first three years of that marriage before Peg was able to stop defending herself from an attack that never came; before she could relax into the easy comfort of loose love. "I over-analyzed. I kept thinking…I don't know how it's gonna happen, but he's gonna start in on me any day now. I was always looking over my shoulder, thinking that if he ever started, I'd be ready for him. I kept looking in drawers for those puzzle pieces, even though they weren't there."

In a small, hidden part of Peg was the belief that physical and psychological violence would follow her into a second marriage. It was me, a small voice would whisper. It was something about me that made Ira punch the top of my head with his fist for taking too many of the bedcovers as I slept. It was something about me that made him roll his eyes in disgust whenever I spoke. It was something about me…and now the same me that turned Ira into a monster is married to Phil. When would Phil's abuse start? What form would it take? And then, slowly, she came to see that there was to be no abuse in this marriage. She could wrap herself in a fluffy cocoon of bedcovers; Phil would simply get out of bed and take another blanket out of the linen closet. He would never abuse her, because he would never abuse anyone. Because Phil, unlike Ira, isn't an abuser. It wasn't me, she finally realized. It wasn't me, after all. It was never about me.

❧ Reflection ❧

The majority of Ira's abuse was what is ordinarily termed "verbal" abuse. I shy away from this term, which summons up trivial visions of yelling. I use the phrase "psychological abuse" to describe the entire range of behaviors — criticism, teasing, sarcasm, swearing, threats, accusations, jealousy, and isolation, among others — employed by an abuser to diminish his victim. "So he yells a little," I hear a popular radio psychologist admonish the distraught woman who has called for advice on how to handle her verbally abusive husband. "What's the big deal? Yell back. Or ignore him." The therapist's offhand, empty reply makes me want to jump out of my skin. True, in a nonabusive marriage, someone is bound to do a little yelling now and then. But neither partner is an identifiable victim or abuser, because neither partner has more power or control than the other. He yells, she yells back, eventually they stop yelling long enough to listen to each other, and it all blows over. In an abusive marriage, the problem is not an occasional angry voice. Psychological abuse, like physical abuse, has nothing to do with anger. It is a means to an end, where the desired end is control.

In 1970, in the married student housing complex known fondly as The Baby Factory, the husbands attended college while their wives were busy producing and raising children. Each morning the men would all go off to class together, returning home in the late afternoon to eat dinner. Meanwhile, the women spent the day juggling their own workload: diapers, laundry, bedmaking, and endless peanut butter sandwiches. The atmosphere was chaotic and comradely: a bustle of activity tending to the assorted needs of infants and toddlers, followed by extended gabfests on the playground or in the laundry room.

One woman's husband was different from the rest. Citing the moral principle of "high standards," he decreed that she spend the entire day cleaning. Not satisfied to merely give orders, he devised a test worthy of a Brothers Grimm fairy tale. Each morning he would hide a tiny pink rubber eraser somewhere in the house. One day it would be balanced on top of the picture that hung in the entryway. Another day it would be tucked under a sofa cushion. When he arrived home, he expected to see the eraser beside his dinner plate. If his wife was performing her proper wifely duty, he reasoned, she would come upon the eraser at some point during the eight hours he expected her to be cleaning.

His wife obeyed her husband — up to a point. Fifteen minutes before he was due home from class, she and all the other young wives would pour into her apartment and begin a frantic search for the eraser. There would be shouts of triumph when it was discovered in a dark corner behind the crib, on the top shelf of the china cupboard, or taped behind the toilet. This communal game of "Hunt the Eraser" was her one act of defiance against the man she had promised to love, honor, and obey.

Twenty-eight years later, they are still married. He is a judge.

There is more to this story. Last year I participated in a quilting class: five women sat around a long table as the teacher showed us how to cut, piece, and assemble. The subject of housecleaning came up, and the teacher decided to entertain us with this story of the "wacky woman" and her "even wackier husband" who lived next door when her husband was in medical school. She was a participant in the daily eraser hunt, and giggled as she described how all the student wives had bamboozled this little Napoleon. My fellow quilters were scornful. "If he were my husband, I'd castrate him," said one. "She must have been a real marshmallow," said another. "I have no respect for women like that. He's sick, but she's even sicker."

I wish I could report that I jumped up and made a speech worthy of Clarence Darrow. I didn't. Everyone was having such a cozy time assembling tidy squares of fabric. It was all so orderly; nobody wanted to hear about the messiness of domestic violence. And who would have believed that a campaign of psychological abuse could be mounted — and won — with a weapon as innocuous as a tiny pink eraser?

Peg married Ira when she was twenty and left when she was twenty-four. An outside observer peering at their marriage during those four years would, I am quite sure, have wondered why Peg put up with Ira's abuse. That observer would very likely have felt disgusted with what appeared to be passivity on her part. Why does she let him get away with the insults? Why does she tolerate the punches?

These are the questions raised by friends and family of a battered woman, exasperated when she remains with her batterer. Yet inaction is not always lethargy. In Peg's case, in the case of many abused women, necessary work is taking place below the surface. Until that work is complete, leaving is unlikely. It may be impossible. It may very well be undesirable. There is a parallel in the insect world. Substantial energy is required for a moth to lift itself in flight. The wing muscles must reach a certain critical temperature before they can contract rapidly enough to move the wings at a rate guaranteed to provide liftoff. Until that temperature is reached, flight is impossible. Before taking off on a cold evening, moths sit quietly, to all appearances inactive, flexing their flight muscles without actually moving their wings until they have worked up enough heat to take off. Then suddenly, with seemingly no effort or warning, their wings flutter and they are gone.

When I was twelve, an enormous luna moth materialized before me one summer evening, illuminated in the beam of our front porch light. Seeing it in graceful flight, I never imagined the effort behind that flight: the time of silent flexing, impatient waiting, until its muscles had warmed enough to move those impossibly oversized celadon wings. On the surface, it would appear that Peg left Ira because he kicked her when she was pregnant. A single turning point. Every action has an equal and opposite reaction. Kick, leave. The reality is more complex. Ira's kick was indeed a turning point, but only because Peg's muscles had been flexing for some time. There were the friends who seemed, on close inspection, to be faintly amused at Ira's pompous pronouncements. There were the lucrative film projects that Ira never quite seemed to be able to bring to fruition. There was the upstairs neighbor who once commented that Ira seemed to be something of a bastard. Just a passing comment, not a lengthy speech, but Peg heard it. Heard it, remembered it, and tucked it into the drawer with the other puzzle pieces.

5
Carolee Curtis

I Bided My Time

*Early in the marriage, I was too immature to recognize
that damage could occur emotionally to my son. But as
Bobby got older, and I matured, then I knew I didn't
want him to be exposed to any more of this. So my job
was to find a way to get free. And then I just started
plotting and biding my time till I was secure enough to
let the plan unfold.*

Like Peg McBride, Carolee Curtis took her time. The first
time she attempted to leave her batterer, she simply ran out of
the house, leaving behind not only all her possessions but also
her ten-year-old son. It is not surprising that she returned
within hours. The next time, she planned carefully. And she
and her son got away safely. A battered woman is more likely
to be seriously injured or murdered in the six months after
she leaves than at any other time during the relationship. Many
women spend months — sometimes years — planning. Like
the prisoners of war in *The Great Escape*, they build tunnels:
cautiously, painstakingly, sometimes no more than a teaspoon-
ful of earth at a time.

For the last four years of their ten-year marriage, Carolee's
husband kept his family isolated in a small house at the edge
of a remote town in Michigan's Upper Peninsula. Carolee was

only allowed to drive the car to the supermarket and back; Frank would scrutinize the odometer to be sure she hadn't made any unauthorized side trips. He would unpack the grocery bags when she returned. Often he would check her purchases against the register receipt, demanding the change from the money he had doled out. She fantasized about getting herself and her son away from Frank, but he kept her too poor to leave. And so Carolee mastered the fine art of embezzlement. Using her only financial resource — the grocery money — she spirited away a dime here, a dollar there. "I was planning ahead. I knew I'd need first and last month's rent, I'd need bus fare to go look for a job, I'd need pantyhose and a haircut." Carolee makes regular donations to the local battered women's shelters. Instead of sending a check, she puts together a care package: a coupon for a haircut at Perfect Look, coupons for Leggs pantyhose, and a one-month Chicago Transit Authority pass. "Listen, it's wonderful to donate money to a shelter. They can buy new furniture or something. But if a woman's looking for a job and she's at a shelter, she has runs in her stockings, her hair is a mess, she doesn't look good, who's gonna hire her?"

Carolee is a large woman in her early fifties, businesslike and competent behind her desk. The window ledge is filled with plants. The walls are filled with framed diplomas, certificates, and awards. She wears a soft wool dress the color of vintage claret, accented with an attractive silk scarf. Her graying hair is cut stylishly short; her pantyhose, I am sure, are impeccable. I do not envy Carolee her job, though she is clearly well suited to it: she is the Director of Patient Services at Chicago City Hospital. When a patient feels mistreated by the hospital administration or the medical staff, Carolee is the one who untangles the accusations and counter-accusations. "I'll get to the bottom of this problem," I can imagine her saying to an irate patient, "but don't you give me any crap." The people she sees in her office are often belligerent; Carolee's secretary watches for trouble and maintains a direct line to hospital security. Now and then, an armed guard has come running to Carolee's office. But Carolee is generally quite capable of keeping explosive situations under control. "They can't scare me," she states firmly. "I've been scared by the expert. These guys down here at CCH are nothing compared to what I had in my life."

Carolee Curtis was twenty when she married Frank Williams. "I'm a Chicago gal...grew up not far from here, went to grade school and high school in the neighborhood. And in high school, the fellow on the next street, he was my eventual husband." Carolee and Frank began dating when they were in the tenth grade. They both participated in school and community musical activities. Carolee played the trumpet. She also sang in her church choir. While Carol's musical ability was better than average, Frank was the star. He led the baritone section in the high school chorus, sang with the Chicago Youth Choir, and was a founding member of the Sweet City Singers, a popular rock-and-roll foursome that performed at local high school dances. "He was my only real boyfriend. He was the best vocalist, and also a star football player. He got a college scholarship for voice and went for two years to college, as did I. Then both of us were recruited into the Army. That was when we got married, so we could go overseas together."

Carolee's mother objected to the marriage. "She said, you know, I had a lot of life to live and why did I want to get married so early? But to me it seemed like the right thing to do. Then about a year later, our son Bobby came along." Bobby was born in Germany, where Frank and Carolee were stationed for eighteen months. She trained as an army nurse. Frank was assigned to the Overseas Army Chorus. Resplendent in red jacket, starched white shirt, and black tuxedo pants, he traveled across Europe performing at military functions and entertaining the troops. "He never really had to be an Army person wearing Army duds," Carolee explains. "He got away with stuff. He was always sort of singled out as this special guy with the great voice."

In hindsight, Carolee realizes that Frank was abusive from the start. At the time, though, she did not understand what was happening. "I was very innocent. So when we were dating he would be forcing me into sexual things that I had never even heard of, and I'd be wondering, but who could you talk to about it? Certainly not the minister. You wouldn't dare bring up such a subject. And then once we got married he started with the slapping, the fighting, the shoving." The chorus traveled often, so Frank's beatings were infrequent. But after each violent outburst, he would make it clear to Carolee that she was to blame. If only the house had been tidier when he came home from one of his tours. If only the checkbook had been balanced properly. If only there had been a full tank of gas in the car. If only Bobby had been freshly bathed and in pajamas. "Dumb fucking fascist pig," Carolee remembers, shuddering as she hears herself repeat the words. "That was his nickname for me. That was what he called me, whenever I made a mistake. Then I was a dumb fucking fascist pig. When we were out in public around the army base, or in front of officers, he would just smile at me and whisper DFFP. Folks probably thought it was a little pet name, but I knew what he meant."

He meant that she had done something wrong. That she would be in trouble once they were alone.

Carolee is an only child who never knew her father. Her mother operated a small day care center in their home so that she could spend sufficient time with her daughter. The two of them lived a calm, orderly life where voices were rarely raised. "I had never seen men shout or be aggressive or be assertive to the point where you had to do what they said you had to do. I didn't know anything about that. So I never did learn to verbally defend myself in a fight or say, 'What are you talking about?' or 'How dare you?' I didn't have much backbone — I didn't know that I *could* have backbone! Frank was mean and he was demanding and I didn't have a clue that it was out of the ordinary, except I thought…if this is what marriage is all about, I sure don't like this."

I find Carolee's self-assessment disturbing. This is a woman who is extremely knowledgeable about domestic violence. She is often invited to lecture on the subject to health professionals at her own and other Chicago area hospitals. In her presentations, she makes it clear to her audience that domestic violence is never the fault of the victim. She would be the first to insist that Frank's curses and slaps had nothing to do with the house, the checkbook, the car, or Bobby's pajamas. "You can't lay a reason to it," she declares firmly, "because there is no reason to be abused." Yet, in the next breath, she holds her childhood up to a strong light, seeking flaws, as though the diplomacy and tact she learned in her mother's home had somehow contributed to her abusive marriage. As though, had she come from a family of angry words and angry fists, she would have mastered ceremonies and incantations that would magically turn a violent man into a peaceful one.

Carolee spent eighteen months in Germany struggling to be an Army wife, a Second Lieutenant nurse, and a mother to Bobby. It was in Germany, she believes, that Frank's violence was fully unleashed. She was not the only one who saw it; an officer on the base once approached her with some concern. Was she aware, he asked, that Frank had a terrible temper? Yes, she replied, but Frank didn't really mean anything by his outbursts. He only acted that way, she assured the officer, if he was provoked. She wishes now that she had been more forthcoming, admitting her fears to both the uneasy officer and to herself. "I didn't understand what he was trying to tell me. I had seen Frank treat me badly, but I thought I was the only one. So, I told the officer that I could handle it. But really, deep inside, I knew I was in trouble. I knew I needed to get out of Germany and back to Chicago."

Carolee describes herself as a dogged person. "My mother taught me the work ethic, and I just didn't know that I *could* stop. I didn't know I could have a nervous breakdown, I didn't know I could take drugs, I didn't know how to drink, I didn't know how to smoke. But I did know how to keep plodding along...so that's what I did. I just plodded along." When their tour of duty ended, neither Carolee nor Frank chose to re-enlist. They moved back to the States, to a suburb just south of Chicago. Carolee hoped that the three of them would be able to settle down to a normal life. Perhaps the rigid structure of military life had been too stressful for Frank. Now that he was a civilian, back on his own home turf, things would surely improve. But Frank began to get into fights, stay out all night, and gamble away his paycheck. He was earning a regular salary as a bank operations manager, but Carolee could never count on his income. They moved often, each apartment smaller and dingier than the last. "It was a nightmare, because he would keep me awake all night, and then I'd have to go to work in the morning exhausted. But I had a good-paying job as a nurse. With his gambling, we needed my income, so I could never call in sick."

I ask the question tentatively, not wanting to offend her or sound judgmental. Frank's violence seems to have escalated in Chicago; was he abusing drugs or alcohol? Carolee is not offended, but she is definite. "Certainly not drugs, and alcohol just modestly. So you would never know when his temper was going to flash. You could never predict, if you blinked wrong or if you walked past him and didn't smile, then it would erupt. It could be over such dumb things, too. He always liked Boston serving, where you use one hand to hold the platter and the other to hold two large serving spoons. You clap them together and you serve off the dish with one hand, which is ridiculous. I don't know where he even got it from; maybe one of those generals he was always entertaining in Germany, but that was what I was supposed to do. And I was just too stupid to tell him to blow it out his ass!"

When Bobby was six, Frank suddenly announced that the three of them were leaving Chicago for good. The city was no place to raise a boy: too crowded, too noisy, too dangerous. He had found a small house in the Upper Peninsula of Michigan. "He sweet-talked me. He told me that life would be great. We could live cheaply up there in the middle of nowhere, so I wouldn't have to work and could be there for Bobby, just like my own mother had been there for me." It was a clever gambit, unerringly aimed at Carolee's single weak spot. She had been feeling guilty about Bobby, especially after she discovered that on days when she worked late, Frank left Bobby alone in the empty apartment. Perhaps, she mused, Frank will calm down once he gets away from Chicago. There won't be as many temptations in a remote corner of Michigan. We can make a fresh start. What Carolee didn't know is that Frank had his own reasons for leaving Chicago, and they had nothing to do with fresh air or wide open spaces. With his inside knowledge of bank operations, he and a friend had managed to embezzle a considerable sum of money from several area businesses. They hadn't been caught — yet — but Frank thought he should get out of town before they were.

The Williams family rented a small house on the outskirts of town. And for the first time in their marriage, Carolee understood what it meant to be isolated. She had neither a car nor any other means of transportation; unlike Chicago, there were no bus lines. She also had no job. In Germany and Chicago, work had been a refuge, a place where she was respected. She had never confided in her colleagues on the nursing staff. But simply being around other people, normal people, had kept her connected to reality. Now she was not a nurse — she was not anybody. She felt herself becoming insubstantial. Ghostlike. Some mornings she would peer at her reflection in the bathroom mirror, as if to assure herself that she was still there.

Since Carolee was no longer bringing home a paycheck, Frank was now fully in control of their finances. "It was demeaning. Like, I would go to the store and come back and he would weigh the grapes. I'll never forget him weighing the grapes. He'd say, 'What did you do, eat some grapes? Let me see your mouth.' Because if I didn't give him the exact right change back, he would think that I was keeping money. Which I was! Dimes so that I could make a phone call some night if I had to get away. And so obviously the money wouldn't be right, it would be ten or fifteen or twenty cents off." The sheer ingenuity of her act puts lie to the stereotype of abused women as helpless, passive creatures. In Michigan, the balance of power in Carolee's marriage had tipped heavily toward her husband. Still, Carolee found ways to claim back some of that power, a dime at a time.

Isolation and poverty might have defeated her. Instead, Carolee became energized. "Up until then, I was just sure somebody would save me from this. I always knew that somebody was gonna come and take care of it. And then I realized that nobody was. It had to be me." Reflection led to action. There was no dramatic turning point, no sudden flash of insight. But slowly, silently, Carolee rebelled. "I used to think very rebellious thoughts. One time I spit on his sandwich, can you believe it? It was just such a release to watch him eat the thing. I would never have killed him, but I used to think up ways of doing it where I wouldn't get caught. I'd imagine him dying, and Bobby and me being free." Carolee's invisible acts of sabotage whittled Frank down in her mind. Diminished, he no longer seemed quite so large, quite so terrifying, quite so invincible. Guided imagery, Olympic athletes call it, as they visualize themselves skimming weightless over the ice or triple somersaulting off the balance beam. Carolee visualized safety. At first, her vision was primarily symbolic. "I developed this coping mechanism. As I'm standing in front of him while he's berating me verbally, I would in my mind take myself with a wheelbarrow and go get bricks and mortar. Then I'd come back in front of him and I would make a brick wall as he was screaming at me. The brick wall preserved my mind so that I felt I wouldn't go crazy…I wouldn't lose my integrity or my soul."

Carolee's first escape attempt was unsuccessful. "I left in the middle of the night. It was raining, I was barefoot, and I had to leave my son there because I couldn't smuggle him out. In my mind, I thought I could take in sewing and mending at a motel, until I had enough money to come back for my son. So there I was, with my purse and my portable sewing machine, walking down the highway, thinking I could convince a motel owner to let me have a free room and then I would take in sewing. I can't even imagine what I could have been thinking." Carolee crept home, wet and weary, before dawn. Frank never even knew she had been away. She felt like a failure, but she had learned an important lesson: to get away from this man, she would have to plan carefully.

Her desire to protect Bobby spurred her on. "Early in the marriage, I was too immature to recognize that damage could occur emotionally to my son.. But as Bobby got older, and I matured, then I knew I didn't want him to be exposed to any more of this. So my job was to find a way to get free. And then I just started plotting and biding my time till I was secure enough to let the plan unfold." Years of Frank's physical and psychological violence had worn down Carolee's self-confidence to the point where she barely believed she would ever break free. But she knew she had to try — and she knew she had to succeed. "After that first time, I knew I couldn't risk it unless I was sure I was gonna get away for good. I wanted to be positive because I knew he was capable of killing me."

Carolee considered her options. A young doctor in the emergency room had treated her three times in the space of five months, carefully documenting her bruised upper arms, her broken nose, her black eye. His kindness and sympathy had made her feel almost human again. The photographs were locked securely in the hospital's files. Should she use this evidence to file a restraining order against Frank? "I thought about it. But I was terrified that I would take him to court, it would be his word against mine, and they'd let him go. And then I think he really would have killed me." She had managed to tuck away enough money for bus fare back to Chicago. Should she and Bobby try to sneak away and hide out at her mother's house? "I thought about it. But I was a grown woman — I didn't want to go running home to momma. It was, like, why do I have to leave? Why can't he leave?" Carolee raises her chin defiantly. "I had these beautiful little Hummell figurines that I had bought in Germany. It might sound silly to some people, but I didn't want to leave them behind. They were mine. Why should he get them?"

Finally, Carolee devised a plan worthy of a Mission Impossible episode; a plan that would get Frank into a courtroom while keeping her safe. She would go to the police — but not with a charge of domestic violence. Frank had not stopped his criminal behavior when he left Chicago. "He became involved in embezzlement again, and I thought well, you know, I can turn him in." Carolee went to the sheriff's office and told them what she knew of Frank's activities. She also told them where he hid the documents that would incriminate him. "It turned out that they had been called by the Chicago police right after we moved up there. They had been keeping an eye on Frank, but had never had any evidence. So they were most interested in what I had to say! They came to the house and photocopied those papers, and when he came home they were all ready to take him in." Frank was brought to trial for grand larceny. He was sentenced to twenty-five years in the penitentiary.

With Frank safely locked away, Carolee felt safe for the

first time in her adult life. She was thirty years old. "I didn't want anything in our life that Frank had touched or sullied. We had a big garage sale, sold our furniture, and started over. It was sort of a rebirth…a new beginning." She and Bobby moved back to Chicago. She obtained a divorce. She went back to work. She also went back to college, ultimately completing a Master's degree in Behavioral Science at Northwestern University. She put herself, as well as Bobby, into therapy. "I didn't want Bobby to ever grow up to be an abuser. I wanted him to have self-esteem and believe that to be a man and a father figure is a good thing." Bobby, Carolee tells me with pride, has grown up to be a fine man. He is a partner with a well-respected Chicago architectural firm. She turns the photograph on her desk to show me her son and his family. An attractive man, woman, and three young girls look back at me.

The stark facts of Carolee's escape and new life might sound as though she blossomed effortlessly into an independent woman of the 1970s. In fact, she tells me, though she was happy to be free of Frank, she was uneasy in her role as a single woman. "I knew how to be married. I knew how to cook, and clean, and iron clothes, but I didn't know how to live the single life." Married in 1963 to her only serious boyfriend, she was unprepared for the easy sexuality of the pre-AIDS years. She relives one particularly embarrassing experience, a comedy of errors made possible only through her innocence. "I decided I would go out, and I asked at the hospital, where does a single woman go to just meet people and enjoy herself? Someone said that I should go to a woman's bar. I thought, that's a great thing! A bar that's just for women! So, by golly, I dressed up in my stockings, my white high heels, my white straw purse and my pink summer dress, and took my pool cue, and off I went. Well, the women there were wearing tank tops, and jeans, and no bras, and the ones playing pool were some really tough cookies. And there I was, looking like a real geek. You know, even after I was there for a few minutes, I still didn't understand what kind of a bar it was, but I sure was told in a hurry!"

The point is, Carolee continues, that when it came to dating, she was a product of her upbringing. "Free love, and all that sex, it just wasn't me. I knew I would be better off if I found a fine man to marry." She met Emory shortly after she moved back to Chicago. They married shortly after her divorce was final. "I certainly did not remarry a man that in any way was abusive. He's so far from that, it's amazing. What I was looking for in a new husband was somebody who was — and I say this with all due respect to Emory — simple and uncomplicated. Frank had been extraordinarily bright in a strange way, but he was a very complex person. I wanted someone who was not jealous, was not competitive with me, and would allow me to evolve." Carolee found exactly that in Emory Curtis. He is a bus driver. She describes him as a straight arrow: he is honest, he is a gentleman, and he brings home a paycheck once a week. He likes meat, potatoes, and gravy for dinner. He has, I am sure, never heard of Boston serving. "He doesn't care what the world budget is, or what's going on with computers or the space program. He just wants his family intact and things peaceful."

Six years ago, Carolee received word that Frank had died. Nobody wanted to claim his body, so she drove to Michigan and completed the necessary paperwork to have him cremated. She decided, out of respect for Bobby, to hold a small memorial service. Frank was, after all, the young man's father. So much time had passed, she felt it was important for her to put aside her own feelings and create a ceremony of farewell. She recalled a tranquil spot by a river, a place where the three of them had occasionally picnicked. These were among their few happy days together. Carolee gathered family and friends beside the river, recited a eulogy for Frank, and poured the contents of the urn into the water. The swift current quickly carried away Frank's ashes. "It was for Bobby's sake, to give some dignity to his father. But later, my son said to me, 'Mom, you don't know this, but I've learned to meditate whenever I get a headache. And in meditation, I used to take myself to that quiet riverbank, and I'd visualize the little swirling eddies and the dabs of sunlight coming through the trees. But now when I think about that place I see my dad come — vroom!!! — right up out of the water. It breaks my reverie and I can't meditate there any more.' And I said to him, 'Oh Bobby, honey, if only I had known, I would have flushed that man right down the toilet!'"

It occurs to me that Frank has vanished from Carolee's life as completely and surely as if she had consigned him to the Chicago sewer system. She and Emory have been happily married for twenty-two years. She is proud of her marriage, proud of her son, and proud of her work at the hospital. Life, she concludes, has been good to her. "I'm not a person that believes in fate, but I know those experiences have allowed me to be successful in what I do now. There's a power inside me. I guess that's the gift of the whole thing. I guess what I'm trying to say is that I don't regret what happened to me. I don't regret it at all. I'm sorry that my life developed and blossomed in my mid-thirties rather than in my twenties. But that's okay, too."

ॐ Reflection ॐ

Asking why a woman stays with an abuser is the sort of question that points inexorably to its own answer. Why does she stay…is she out of her mind? …is she some sort of a masochist? …is she too blind to see what he's doing to her? Carolee was none of these. Why, then, did she stay with Frank for ten years? The answer only becomes clear when the question is reframed. Instead of asking about Carolee, ask about Frank. What tactics did Frank use that got in the way of her leaving?

Framed this way, the answer is starkly clear: Frank held all the power. He controlled the finances. He controlled where she went and whom she saw. Not only did he control her with money and isolation; he also controlled her with brute force. When her injuries required a trip to the emergency room, he saw to it that she rarely was alone with a nurse or a doctor. Finally, the most effective of Frank's tactics was emotional destruction. He had convinced her that she was so worthless, so stupid, so ugly that if she left him, she was bound to fail. "Just try to make it without me," he would taunt. "You'll fall flat on your fat ass. You'll end up on the streets."

Until Carolee found a way to wrest that power away from Frank, she was — understandably — stuck. Perhaps she could have run away sooner than she did. But what would have been the probable outcome? If she had tried to take Bobby with her, she had the quite rational fear that Frank would hunt her down. She might have left Bobby behind, but what sort of an option was that? Suppose Carolee had managed to get herself and Bobby safely away, improbably hitching a ride out of town, making her way to a new city where Frank might, if Carolee was lucky, not look for them. Then there would have been the practical realities of living. She was a trained nurse, but she had been out of the work force for four years. What if she was unable to find a job immediately? Where would she and Bobby sleep? How would they eat?

Framed this way, it is not surprising that Carolee stayed for ten years. Rather, it is surprising — even impressive — that she ever managed to escape.

There is a power inherent in our possessions. Under some circumstances, they become touchstones. Originally a flint-like stone used to test the purity of gold by the streak left on the stone when rubbed by the metal, a touchstone has come to mean a test or criterion for determining the quality or genuineness of a thing. Carolee's Hummell figurines were touchstones. "It might sound silly to some people," she said with a slightly defensive tone, "but I didn't want to leave them behind. They were mine." Exactly. They were hers. Frank had everything else: the car, the money, the physical strength, the decision-making power. Carolee's unwillingness to leave her Hummell pieces had nothing to do with their monetary value. The delicate ceramic figurines, bought with her own salary when she was a young Army nurse, helped her remember who she was.

Possessions can help us define ourselves. Clearing them out can be a form of exorcism and, consequently, a step toward healing. "I didn't want anything in our life that Frank had touched," Carolee declared, as though his books, his coffee cup, his footstool had soaked up Frank's negative energy like thirsty sponges. On a rational level, Carolee knew perfectly well that no evil demons lurked among Frank's paraphernalia. The demons, if they existed at all, were safely behind bars with Frank. But as she organized her garage sale, as she carried each item out of the house, placed it carefully on her driveway, affixed a price tag, and sent it on its way, she felt herself becoming thistledown-light. By the end of the day, she was practically floating.

When I left Melvin, I moved to a snug one-bedroom apartment on West End Avenue. I could, I suppose, have laid claim to half our personal effects: furniture, linen, dishes, cookware, and decorative knickknacks. I didn't. I left with my clothes, my graduate school texts, and two items I knew for an absolute fact that Melvin had never touched: the ironing board and the vacuum cleaner. The popular song that winter was "50 Ways to Leave Your Lover," Paul Simon's words so perfectly apt as to make me almost believe he had penned them exclusively for my benefit. I sang the lyrics softly to myself as I distributed my few belongings about the empty, welcoming apartment. "Hop on the bus, Gus; you don't need to discuss much. Just drop off the key, Lee. And get yourself free."

6
Becky Pepper

I Balanced the Fears

He said that I wasn't a proper mother for his son. That he was gonna take Ben away from me and hide him in a place I'd never find him. So now it was like, okay, I'm gonna have to balance the fears.

Becky Pepper does not look like your average fifty-year-old social worker. For one thing, her hair is purple; or if not quite purple, then definitely a vibrant maroon. With her bright fuchsia sweater and her dragonfly-green eyeshadow, she makes quite a picture as she leads me down the narrow corridor to her office. I walk beside her, a dim shadow in my sedate uniform of black shirt and pants. Her office is a jumble of books, file folders, journals, and computer disks. As we sit, she sweeps a mound of papers from a corner of her desk to make room for our coffee cups. She puts her elbows on the desktop and leans forward, her head on her hands, a look of intense concentration on her face. A perfect social worker pose. Then she begins to speak. The professional poise and confidence peel away, revealing a twenty-year-old who made several bad choices.

Becky's first bad choice was to become pregnant. Her second was to marry the baby's father. Becky married Leonard DeGiulio in 1968. She was ten years his junior; too young, she confesses, to know the difference between being in love and being horny. Although the circumstances of their marriage were slightly embarrassing (more so to Becky's mother than to Becky herself), Becky was delighted to be a wife and expectant mother. Until Leonard, the romantic, attractive man who promised to be Ozzie to Becky's Harriet, changed.

Within a few weeks of their marriage Becky realized that she was in trouble. It began with makeup. Why was she wearing all that stuff on her face? Becky was confused. She had been wearing makeup since she was ten. "It was the sixties. It was California. My girlfriends and I were into heavy mascara, lots of eyeliner, tons of foundation. It was the style, and besides, I liked it. So I didn't pay any attention to him." And then one day Leonard pushed her against the wall. Hadn't he asked her politely to stop wearing makeup? If she wasn't wearing it for him, who was she wearing it for? "Right away, I had this feeling like, uh-oh, there's something very wrong here. You know, I didn't ever like the way my father behaved toward us kids when I was growing up, but I never saw anything like this. Never."

In retrospect, Becky concedes that her father could have been nicer to his wife and three children. "He would work all day. Then he would come home, sit in his chair, smoke his cigar, read his book, and play with the dog (but never us kids). Meanwhile, my mother would do everything for him." This was not, she emphasizes, an abusive home; just your average patriarchy that reigned in most suburban homes during the years following World War II. As a feminist and a social worker, Becky wishes she could send a message back three decades to the 1950s, to the woman her mother was then. "I would tell her the same thing I tell my patients today. It's not appropriate to have someone talk to you this way. Women are not genetically predisposed to do the dishes. Marriage is supposed to be a partnership."

Becky's father might have been remote and overbearing, but he was nothing like her husband. After the incident with the makeup, Leonard's campaign to control Becky quickly escalated. First it was the length of her hair. Too long. Then it was the length of her mini-skirts. Too short. Eventually, Leonard didn't even rely on the excuse of Becky's actions to make him hit her. She pushes her chair back from her desk, lifts her arm, and swats the air viciously to illustrate her point. "It started out with 'I told you not to do that (smack).' Pretty soon it was 'Don't you dare look at me that way (smack).' "

Their son Ben was born six months after they were married. When the baby was three weeks old, Becky tentatively suggested that she take Ben to visit his grandmother for a few days. Though the trip was presented as a short visit, Becky had other plans. Once safely at her parents' house, she hoped to extend the weekend into a permanent separation. Leonard seemed able to read her mind. She could go, he warned ominously, but she'd better be back by Sunday night. "Because if you don't, you're not the only one who's gonna get hurt." Though Leonard wasn't specific, Becky understood his veiled threat. Becky's youngest sister Tracey is mentally retarded; she was seven at the time, and completely defenseless. Anyone who knew Becky knew that Tracey was her weak spot. Whenever Leonard expressed his intention to make someone else pay for Becky's behavior, he always specifically mentioned her sister.

Leonard seemed to sense that Becky was more frightened of what he would do to others than what he would do to her. He learned to manipulate her natural inclination to protect the small and helpless; an inclination that led her, not many years later, to become a social worker. A dramatic example was the time Leonard tried to kill the cat. Becky shudders as she describes the episode. "I was nursing the baby, and I guess I must have looked at Leonard in a way he didn't like. He picked up the cat and started choking it…she was struggling in his hands, and her eyes bugged out and got bloodshot. I thought: Omigod, he's gonna kill that cat." As the cat squirmed in his grasp, Leonard grimly fixed his gaze on Becky. The message was unmistakable. This time, it was the cat. Next time, it might be Becky.

After that, Becky thought long and hard about leaving. She took careful stock of her situation. Finances weren't a problem: she had a job, so she could certainly afford to rent a little apartment where she and Ben could live. But she was worried that Leonard would track her down. Or, worse, that he would harm Tracey. A man who could strangle a cat, she reasoned, would be capable of anything. Afraid to stay, afraid to leave, she felt frozen in place. Then one night Leonard came home from work and made an announcement. He had been giving it a lot of thought, he said calmly, and had come to the conclusion that she was an unfit mother. Becky could tell that Leonard had been drinking. Had he slurred his words, thrown things, or shouted, she probably would have dismissed his threat. But the icy complacency of his voice terrified her. "He said that I wasn't a proper mother for his son. That he was gonna take Ben away from me and hide him in a place I'd never find him. So now it was like, okay, I'm gonna have to balance the fears."

Leonard was a lab technician at a hospital. In those days, narcotic drugs were not tracked as carefully as they are today. Employee theft was perhaps not common, but certainly fairly effortless for those who were so inclined. Leonard had been stealing Nembutal from the hospital for some time. Every evening after dinner he would empty a capsule into a highball and sit hazily in front of the TV set, eventually nodding out on the sofa. That night, as Leonard serenely explained why she had given him no choice but to kidnap their son, Becky actually found herself contemplating murder. "I recall thinking, you know, if I just opened a few more capsules into his highball, he would drink it. It tasted like poison anyway. He would never know...and he would die. Everyone at work knew he raided the drug cabinet. It would be a drug overdose, and who would ever suspect me? I thought about it for a long time, but I just couldn't bring myself to do it. So instead what I did is, I escaped."

Unlike Carolee Curtis, Becky could not bide her time. She had to take immediate action. She waited until the highball and Nembutal took effect. When Leonard began to snore, she quietly began to pack. "I had one bag. I shoved as much baby stuff into it as I could fit. I threw on a black turtleneck and sweatpants, gathered up all the money I could find, and — baby under one arm, bag under the other — I ran out of the house." Becky ran three blocks to a gas station and called her girlfriend Rosemarie from the pay phone. She acknowledges that she was luckier than many abused women: because she had only been with Leonard for about a year, she still had girlfriends. He had forbidden her to maintain contact with them, but he was out of the apartment often enough that she was able to remain in touch with her closest friends by phone.

Chances are excellent that, had she remained with Leonard much longer, he would have managed to sever these connections.

Rosemarie drove to the gas station and parked in the darkness behind the building. Huddled in the back seat, ready to duck out of sight if Leonard improbably awakened and came looking for his wife and son, the two friends problem-solved together. Where could Becky go to be safe from Leonard? Not to Becky's parents' house. It was the first place Leonard would look. And it was where Tracey lived; Tracey, whom Leonard had promised to hurt. Not to Rosemarie's house...she loved Becky dearly, but didn't want to risk her own life. Eventually they called Becky's uncle: her father's brother Mike. A large, powerful man, Mike ate guys like Leonard for lunch. Rosemarie drove Becky to Mike's house, where she and the baby spent the next month hiding out. As a social worker, Becky has had enough experience with battered women to realize how fortunate she was. "I was lucky that I had someplace to go to. And people who were willing to take me in and willing to deal with the threats and also financially support me."

Becky was fortunate in another way: as far as she knows, Leonard did not stalk her. He certainly didn't make good on his threats to hurt her or her family. But she knows full well that he could have; that many men do. Instead, Leonard switched gears. Since intimidation hadn't worked, he tried to manipulate Becky with tears. Perhaps his plan was to exploit Becky's tendency to protect the defenseless. Perhaps he reasoned that if he seemed weak, Becky would take pity on him. He couldn't get to Becky directly — she and Ben were safely ensconced with Uncle Mike, and Uncle Mike wasn't about to let him near them. Instead, Leonard took to calling Becky's parents. He hadn't meant to hurt her. He would never do it again. He loved her deeply. He wanted her back. Her parents dutifully passed the messages along, but Becky was unimpressed. She was out. It was over.

Though some abused women leave several times before they are able to end the relationship permanently, Becky never looked back. She filed for, and was awarded, a divorce and sole custody of their son. (Ben, who is 28 now, has no relationship with his father.) She did not ask for child support or alimony; she just wanted her freedom. To an outsider, Becky might have looked like a failure: a twenty-two year old with a baby to support. But she didn't see it that way. She was alive, and she was safe. She has remained safe for nearly thirty years. "But I've gotta tell you, it was years before I really believed it. Every time I walked out my door, I thought...well, just because he hasn't snapped and killed me so far, it doesn't mean that he won't." Leonard's drug and alcohol addiction steadily worsened. He drifted in and out of substance abuse treatment programs. Now and then one of his doctors would call Becky, looking for information about his prior drug abuse history. She cooperated up to a point, but set boundaries: she would tell the doctors what she could, but she would neither see nor speak to her ex-husband. About ten years ago, Becky heard that Leonard had been arrested for a hit-and-run while intoxicated. She wasn't particularly surprised.

As I look at the vibrant woman seated across from me, I wonder if her story disproves my notion that abuse always has an aftermath. Becky looks so together — so in charge of her life. True, she worried about her safety for a few years. But it seems as though she essentially walked away unscathed. She only stayed with Leonard for a year. Many women, myself included, stay for much longer. So perhaps, given that her abusive marriage occupied only one-fiftieth of her life, there hasn't been an aftermath? Don't you believe it. To this day, Becky cannot be in a room with anyone who is drinking. "It doesn't matter who they are, it doesn't matter how well I know them, it doesn't matter how benign a person they are. My husband is the nicest, gentlest man, but if he has two beers, I panic. Which I recognize is completely irrational. He hardly ever drinks…if he had three beers he'd be asleep. But if I see him reaching for a beer, I get this panicky thing in my chest. Leonard hit me when he was sober, but he hit me harder when he was drunk." Becky shakes her head ruefully. "I don't think I'll ever get past it, if twenty-seven years later I'm still having trouble."

There is a stereotype that, even when a woman manages to escape from her abuser, she immediately turns around and finds herself another. Like all stereotypes, this one has some basis in fact while obscuring the truth. Some women do move from one abusive relationship into another. Some women don't. And some women — like Becky — find themselves somewhere in the middle. When Becky was 24, she made one more bad choice. She moved in with Art. He was not abusive, but in retrospect Becky admits that he was no prize. "It isn't that he was awful, but he would manipulate me. He knew how to make me feel guilty, make me feel sorry for him, and kind of get me to go along with his way." It wouldn't have happened, Becky says, had she been a stronger personality at the time. But she was still learning the lesson that women could be strong.

One of the ways Art would manipulate Becky was to threaten to leave. For four years, this technique worked admirably. "If we can't resolve this, I'll move out," he would warn, and she would scramble to mend the rift. Finally, though, Becky reached her limit. She was twenty-eight, she had completed her social work degree, and she felt a sense of accomplishment. She recognized how strong she was — how strong, in fact, she always had been. So she sat Art down and laid it on the line. "I'm just really, really tired of hearing that. So this is what I think. The next time you say it, you'd better mean it, because you're out of here." Which is precisely what happened. In the midst of an argument, Art threatened to move his things out of the apartment. Becky looked him straight in the eye and said, "Okay, pal...time to go." Art was stunned when he realized that Becky really meant it. It took her months to ease him out of the apartment; he was like gum stuck to the bottom of her shoe. She finally had to resort to the time-honored tradition of putting all his possessions on the landing and changing the locks.

Once Art was gone, Becky felt that her life had really started. "I started having some really fun years. I felt terrific about myself. Powerful. It was the 1970s, before AIDS, and I had a harem of men. I learned how to manipulate men, rather than having them manipulate me." I can't help giggling at the image of her "harem of men." In my mind's eye I picture her reclining on a silk couch whose purple and green cushions precisely match her hair and eyeshadow, while handsome bare-chested studs place gifts at her velvet-slippered feet. I share my vision with Becky, and the two of us crack up. It strikes me, though, that these "party" years were another sort of aftermath; a way of doing unto men before they had a chance to do unto her. Does she think, I ask, that she needed to keep men at a distance? She hadn't thought of it that way before, but concedes that I may have a point. "I was having a blast, but I wasn't taking any shit. I guess I sort of went to the other end of the spectrum. Don't raise your voice at me. Don't tell me what to do. I decided that if you don't take care of yourself, you can't depend on anyone else to do it."

After five years of what she calls "fun and games," Becky met a man who was different. The first time Richard Hill asked her out, she refused. He didn't seem to be her type; somehow, she couldn't see him ensconced in her harem. Eventually he talked her into dating him, "...but it was actually difficult getting used to someone being nice to me, treating me respectfully. It sounds bizarre, but I was uncomfortable with that much niceness." As she spent more time with Richard, she took a second look at the men she had been dating during the past five years. They were nice guys. They had treated her perfectly well. But she hadn't let a single one of them get close to her.

Was there something about Richard, I ask Becky, which convinced her to stop protecting herself? Or was it perhaps the reverse: she met a good man at a time in her life that she was able to appreciate one? She isn't sure. But she agrees that dating Richard was a new experience: an intimate relationship with a man who wasn't out to control her. Finding peace had been important to her, though she hadn't been aware that she needed it until she had it. A case in point was the weekend she borrowed Richard's car to visit her brother in San Diego. An hour into the trip, the car broke down, leaving her high and dry in the middle of the Santa Monica Freeway. Becky hitched a ride to a gas station where she dialed Richard's number. Her hand shook and her shoulders tensed as she braced herself for the blast of anger she knew would come the moment he heard her voice. "I said, 'Oh, Richard, I broke your car,' which is an indication in itself, isn't it? Not 'Your car broke, dammit,' but

'I did it.' Like I got into the carburetor and did it on purpose, right? So I'm ready for the onslaught, and I hear him say, 'Oh my God, Becky, I'm so sorry my car broke on you!' And I'm looking at the phone going, 'He's not mad at me. What the hell is wrong with him?' You know, that's really what I was thinking."

Becky and Richard dated for three years. His first marriage had ended in an amicable divorce; when his ex-wife returned to her native South Africa, he took sole custody of their son and daughter. By the time Becky and Richard married in 1986, her son Ben and his new siblings were all in their mid to late teens. Becky made sure all three children learned the message of nonviolence and respect for others. "I think it's so important for us to teach our children how to behave. I spent a lot of time with Richard's daughter when she was in her teens, talking about self-esteem and her right to decide what she wants and when she wants it. I talked to her about all the foolish things boys will say to try to manipulate you." Her son and stepson were taught a slightly different lesson. "I told them how easy it is for them to hurt people both physically and emotionally. I made sure they understood that they're special because of who they are, but they're not special just because they're men. Having a penis doesn't make you better — it just means you're that variety of human being."

Becky firmly believes that domestic abuse will only end when there are fairly significant changes in our society. She thinks aloud, more to herself than to me, as she absently plays with her coffee cup. "If we continue to teach our children that men are special, if we continue to not punish men for raping and pillaging just because they're really great athletes, we're not going anyplace as a society."

❧ Reflection ❧

Unlike Peg McBride, Becky did not spend time mulling over Leonard's good and bad points or contemplating her options. Unlike Carolee Curtis, she did not have the luxury of planning an orderly escape. She ran, because she felt she had no other choice. She ran to protect herself; she ran to protect her son. Operating purely on instinct, she kept herself as safe as she possibly could, under the circumstances. Still, Becky would be the first to acknowledge that leaving a batterer with no safety plan in place is dangerous at best, fatal at worst. If she had confronted Leonard, or attempted to get away while he was sober enough to stop her, the outcome might have been tragically different.

What Becky has in common with Peg and Carolee is the fact that getting away from an abusive man is always a complex process. Despite the common image of a battered woman as a weak, passive, rather helpless creature, women in abusive relationships generally understand the realities of their situation far better than they are given credit for. Often, as in Becky's case, they are pulled in many directions. Becky was torn between the undeniable reality of two equally powerful fears: her fear of Leonard and her fear for her younger sister, Tracey. Had I been in Becky's situation, I would have been hard-pressed to make my escape, knowing that I was putting my family in peril. I would, I believe, have done just what Becky did. I would have hunkered down for a while.

The unqualified support of Becky's friends and family should not be underestimated. I can imagine alternative scenarios. She might, perhaps, have had no one to turn to. Because she had only been with Leonard for a year, she was not yet as isolated as most abused women. She was still in touch with her girlfriend, Rosemarie. She might, perhaps, have had no safe place to hide. How many battered women have an Uncle Mike, willing to offer a safe haven and plant themselves in front of it like a stubborn badger? She might, perhaps, have had parents who did not understand what she was escaping from. What would have happened if, when Leonard began crying to Becky's parents, they had urged her to give her marriage one more try "for the sake of the baby"?

On December 25, 1975, I turned twenty-seven and told Melvin the marriage was over. The following week, I invited my parents to lunch and reported the news: they were losing a son-in-law, and regaining a daughter. During the two years since Melvin and I had moved back to New York, my parents and I had resumed some of the intimacy that we had lost in my early years of marriage. Melvin no longer ridiculed my Sunday evening phone calls, my occasional trips to Bloomingdale's with my mother — or, if he did, I no longer noticed. Still, as I slid a quiche into the oven and tossed a green salad, I felt just the tiniest bit jumpy. My parents had been happily married for thirty years; would they be disappointed that I was bringing my eight-year marriage to an end? My announcement would surely take them by surprise. They had seen no emotional fireworks, no dramatic showdown, because there had been none. Like Peg and Carolee, like many abused women, the process of disentangling myself had been conducted largely in the privacy of my mind.

Melvin and I were separating, I told them, my voice calm despite my twitching stomach. I had found an apartment. I was moving out at the end of the month. For a brief moment that seemed to last an hour, they were both very quiet. Then my father broke the silence. "How do you feel?" he asked carefully. Until the word popped from my mouth, I had not known what it would be. "Relieved," I replied without a moment's hesitation.

My parents smiled at me across the table. Their eyes spoke volumes; their words spoke the rest. "If you're relieved, then you're doing the right thing. We're behind you one hundred percent. What can we do?"

Section III
After It's Over, It's Not Over

Leaving is not the end of the story. Abuse profoundly colors a woman's life. Even if she manages to escape safely and to rebuild her life, there is always an aftermath. Most women who get out of abusive relationships do not realize this. They think they are the only ones who suffer flashbacks. They wonder why they cannot sleep — why they cannot trust. A woman abused has lost her faith in a benign universe. She has learned that the world is not a safe place. She has learned to be suspicious.

An animal that has survived the terror of a forest fire recognizes the acrid smell of smoke faster than one who has not. A woman who has survived an abusive relationship becomes hyper-vigilant, determined to protect herself from further danger. Each of the stories in this section describes the legacy of domestic abuse.

7
Whitney Benson

Will the Scars Ever Heal?

*Guys bring me flowers sometimes when they come to
pick me up for a date and I'm just like, "Oh, no!"
Because to me flowers mean he's either going to do
something bad to me, or he already has.*

She is an attractive young woman — tall, slim, and poised
— with a sweet contralto voice and an inviting smile. When
she was a little girl she appeared in a few television ads and
dreamed of becoming a fashion model or an actress. By the
time she entered college she had settled on a new, equally competitive goal: broadcast journalism. Last summer, after
completing her freshman year at Utah State University, Whitney
applied for an internship at a local television station. The
woman in the personnel office shook her head with prim dis-
approval. "You have too many scars, dear. We can't take you."
Her voice wobbles as she relives the memory. "I just died. I got
in my car and drove a block, but I had to pull over. I was an
emotional disaster. I thought...I cannot *believe* this. I cannot
believe that this is going to hold me back."

Today is the second time I have met Whitney, and I am
startled. Does she have scars? I lean forward to get a better
look as she points out what she deftly covers each morning
with flesh-toned concealer and heavy base makeup. There, on

her chin, I see a faint horizontal line, three inches long. There, by the corner of her left eye, I see a delicate web of cross-hatching. Now that I know where to look for her scars, I wonder how I could have missed them.

Whitney sat in the seat beside mine in the auditorium of the Utah State Capitol, a fellow participant at an awards ceremony for community volunteers. We began chatting during the morning coffee break. I learned that she fields hotline calls at the Teen Rape Crisis Center; she learned that I lead domestic violence training programs at local area businesses. "Why domestic violence training?" she asked me. Brushing bits of powdered sugar and doughnut crumbs from my lap, I quickly summarized my life history. "Why the rape crisis hotline?" I countered. She told me about Brad, the boy who manipulated, tormented, and ultimately, when she broke off the relationship, brutally raped her. The next week Whitney called me. She knew I was writing a book about women who survived abusive marriages. But what about dating violence? She wanted to tell me her story. And I wanted to hear it.

Whitney Benson was born in 1977, the year I turned thirty, two years after I ended my marriage to Melvin. She met Brad Christiansen when she was fourteen. Brad was sixteen, a high school sophomore and the town catch. He was a football hero. He drove a jet-black BMW convertible. He was the undisputed leader of Green Valley High School's coolest clique. Although such cliques are present in high schools across America, they have a special significance in a small southern Utah town like Green Valley. Teen society there revolves around the twin hubs of high school and church. In Green Valley, the only girls with an active social life are the ones who are both Mormon and members of the school's smart set. Whitney's religion was not a problem; like ninety percent of the town, she and her family are observant Mormons. Her popularity seemed equally secure. Teenagers begin pairing off early in Green Valley. These are not official dates, since Mormon girls are technically not supposed to date until they turn sixteen. Nevertheless, in junior high school, when Whitney and her girlfriends went to parties, basketball games, or Saturday afternoon movies, there were always an equal number of boys present to buy them popcorn, hold their hands, and escort them home. "Little boyfriends," she calls them. Unimportant, except as a measure of her desirability. As Whitney prepared to graduate from junior high school, though, she worried a bit. Group dates and the easy flirtations of junior high school were one thing. What if high school was different? The older students appeared self-assured and sophisticated. Would she measure up?

So that spring, when Brad asked her out, Whitney was ecstatic. If she were to become Brad's girlfriend, she would have instant credibility among the socially savvy group who seemed to run the school. She spent the day getting ready. She fussed over her hair and makeup. She changed outfits at least once an hour. At six o'clock she heard the sound of Brad's BMW pulling up to the curb in front of her parents' house. She waited for him to ring the bell, but he honked the horn impatiently. "It felt more like a car pool than a date, but I ran out the door and got in. Then the first thing he said to me was, 'Oh. Is *that* what you're gonna wear?' So I knew I had picked the wrong outfit, and I felt just awful."

Whitney's description of their first date would be comical if I didn't know the rest of her story. "He acted like he was taking me to the fanciest restaurant in town and you know where we ended up? Denny's! Then he told me I could order whatever I wanted, so I asked for fried chicken strips. But he said, 'You can't eat that! Look at you, you're so fat right now, that would only make it worse.' I had heard that sometimes on a date the guy will order for you, so I didn't like to argue with him. When the waitress came out he said, 'She wants a plain salad...just lettuce, don't put any dressing on it, no carrots, no cucumbers, just lettuce. And I want it in a really small bowl, don't bring her a big bowl.' Then he asked if I wanted anything to drink. I realized that it was more of a test, you know, and I was supposed to say no, but I asked for a root beer. He shook his head impatiently. 'No, you'll have water, and lots of it.' That was the start. From the very first time I went out with Brad, I was on his diet. They say you are what you eat, don't they? When I was dating him I guess I was a head of lettuce and a glass of water!"

Now, five years later, Whitney can see that all the signs of Brad's appetite for control were right there in front of her, as unambiguous as a bowl of iceberg lettuce. At age fourteen, though, she had no standard against which to measure his behavior. He had ordered a meal for her...but perhaps that was what all guys did. He hadn't liked her outfit...but she probably hadn't chosen wisely. He had criticized her weight...but what teenager doesn't examine her hips in despair every time she passes a mirror? As Brad drove her back to her parents' house, Whitney replayed the evening. She had just gone out with the most popular boy in town. Had she had a good time? Brad came into the house and spent a few minutes chatting with Donelle, Whitney's mother. Donelle was impressed with Brad's manners and appearance. She told Whitney what a cute couple the two of them made. She hoped Whitney had enjoyed her date. And so Whitney assumed she probably had. After all, everyone in town had seen her on the arm of Mr. Joe Cool. Her mother approved. Her girlfriends were envious. What more could she possibly want? "Lucky me," she thought to herself. "Everybody wants to be me."

High school started, and Whitney was an immediate success. She hung out with Brad's friends: the athletes, the cheerleaders, the select group of wealthy, well-dressed, sophisticated juniors and seniors who were the arbiters of social status at Green Valley High School. Whitney was the only sophomore in the group, her parents' finances were comparatively modest, but this posed no problem; she was, after all, Brad's girlfriend.

Within a few months, though, Whitney wasn't entirely sure she wanted to be Brad's girlfriend. True, she enjoyed riding to school in his BMW convertible and wearing his letter sweater. She joined the drill team so she could cheer for him at football games. She always had a date for the post-game dance. But there was something about Brad's behavior that felt wrong, though Whitney could not put a name to what disturbed her. In late October, they met to plan their costumes for the school's annual Halloween dance. Brad had definite ideas about what Whitney should wear. Five months of his lettuce-and-water diet had plunged Whitney's weight well below 100 pounds. Her size three clothes hung in folds around her. This, Brad insisted, wasn't good enough. At five feet six inches, she should weigh no more than 90 pounds; 85 would be even better. The solution was obvious: Whitney would have to wear a costume that disguised her rolls of fat. "We went to the thrift shop and he picked out the biggest outfit they had. The pants were too big even for my dad. The shirt and jacket were enormous. When I put everything on I just looked obese. And I was so confused…why would he dress me like that? Why? I didn't get it. All night at the dance he was, like, 'Don't eat that, pudgy!' He teased me at the table when the whole group of us went out to dinner: 'Look at her, just eating lettuce, trying to get skinny, hee hee hee!' But he was the one who kept telling me to eat lettuce. I was starving, he was telling me I was fat, and then he was criticizing me for dieting. I didn't know what I was supposed to do."

By the next morning Whitney had figured out what she was supposed to do: she broke up with Brad. She was tired of his starvation diet, his carefully crafted insults, his choking kisses, and his disturbing habit, when angry, of holding her wrists and forcing her to her knees until she apologized. She told him she never wanted to see him again. She walked to school, refused to take his phone calls, and ignored him at football games. Her parents were mystified. Brad was such a charming boy. The Christiansens were a good Mormon family, known in the community as generous contributors to local charities. Why on earth had she stopped seeing him? Whitney shrugged noncommittally, unwilling to reveal Brad's dark side, certain they would not understand. She did attempt to confide in her friends, but their response was swift and firm: she was a liar. Brad wasn't like that. And Whitney…well, Whitney was simply Brad's ex-girlfriend, no longer worth bothering with.

For the next few months, high school became a pretty dreary place. So when Brad began showing up at her parents' house with flowers and gifts, Whitney found it increasingly difficult to turn him away. "Why did I go back? Everyone always asks me that. Because he was different. He changed. The books about domestic violence talk about the honeymoon stage. Well, Brad was ideal in the honeymoon stage. He was gentle. He was sweet. He gave me presents. I still have buckets of jewelry that he gave me; I can't stand to look at it, I can't touch it, but at the time it made me feel like a princess. And then, of course, there was a lot of pressure from his family, my family, and our friends to get back together. After a while, I thought they must be right."

Whitney told herself that breaking up with Brad had done him a world of good. She had made her point: unless he treated her properly, he would lose her. For several months Brad remained on his best behavior. Then the rigid control started again, more bizarre and frightening than before. "It was like he only wanted me when he couldn't have me. Once he was sure of me, he just wanted to torture me." Brad took pleasure in torture and seemed to have a talent for it. Anna, governess to the King of Siam's children in "The King And I," sings the delightful "Getting To Know You" to establish a relationship of trust with her new students. In a funhouse-mirror distortion of Anna's song, Brad used what he had gotten to know about Whitney to devise an ever-changing menu of punishments. He tapped into her fears, her weaknesses, even her allergies. "I am allergic to pepper: it gives me hives and I can't breathe. He would fry sausage with tons and tons of pepper. He'd say 'I know you're hungry…eat this.' Of course I was hungry! He had me on his diet, and I was starving. But I would tell him I couldn't eat it, that I'd be really, really sick. He'd just stuff it into my mouth and laugh. One time I refused and he said, 'Well, then, take the pan.' The pan was hot and full of sausage grease; he swung it right at my head. That's the day I got this scar on my chin." The next morning Brad left two dozen long-stemmed pink roses on Whitney's homeroom desk. Her girlfriends gushed. No one mentioned the angry red wound.

We return to the subject of Whitney's scars. Some, like the sausage pan, were, if not accidental, at least unplanned. Others were — there is no other word for it — deliberate mutilation. "He's a lot bigger and stronger than me. He would hold my two wrists in his left hand so I couldn't get away. Then he'd scratch his name on different parts of my body. That was his big thing: to claim me as his property. I'm sure if I had been old enough, he would have taken me to a tattoo parlor and had them tattoo his name on me. Thank God you have to be eighteen in this state! But it's sad: even though I finally got him out of my life, I'm left with all these scars. I'm so afraid that when I finally do get married, my husband will ask me why I have this other man's name all over my body. It's his full name, Bradley Willis Christiansen, right across my inner thighs. I hate it that Brad will always have his name on me, like I'm still his property, like he's still here. I hate that worst of all."

Whitney never knew what would spark one of Brad's torture sessions. But her weight was always a handy excuse. "He would tell me, 'You're not skinny enough. If you were skinnier, I wouldn't have to punish you.' So I'd try to get skinnier and skinnier and skinnier. But it was never enough." Whitney finds it nearly unbearable to look at her photographs from that time. Her weight had dropped to 89 pounds. Her hair was thin, her nails brittle, her eyes lusterless. "I had no shape at all. And even worse, I had no energy. It was like he was trying to make me disappear."

In a way, Whitney actually had disappeared. It was as though she and Brad were trapped in an opaque bubble. Nobody around them seemed to see what he was doing to her. Either that, or they didn't find his behavior at all peculiar. Once she stood with Brad and his father on the second-floor landing of his family's house. Brad said something, she contradicted him, he pushed, and she tumbled to the bottom of the stairs. She landed full force on her right arm, her wrist bent at an awkward angle beneath her. Brad and his father watched silently from the top of the staircase. She lay still for a few moments, wondering what she was supposed to do. She remembers thinking that if anyone had been pushed down the stairs in her house the entire Benson family would have been in an uproar. "It's okay, isn't it?" his father called down to her. "Get up. Show me." She slowly mounted the stairs, attempting to wiggle her fingers. "I think it might be broken," she sobbed. Mr. Christiansen roughly forced her hand back and forth. "No, you're fine. If it was broken I couldn't move it like this. See? It's nothing to make a big deal over." Perhaps it's not a big deal, she mused. After all, his father didn't act as though Brad had done anything out of the ordinary. As Brad drove Whitney home, he coached her on an explanation for her swollen wrist. Her parents listened sympathetically as Brad tenderly packed ice around their daughter's hand and told them the story of poor Whitney's accident during drill team practice. He was so convincing that even Whitney began to believe him.

On another occasion, Whitney and Brad became invisible to a crowd of several hundred people. Six movies play in Green Valley's cinema complex, providing sufficient variety to please toddlers to teenagers to grandparents. People line up early on weekend nights. As Whitney and Brad stood in line with everyone else, he asked her which of the six movies she wanted to see. The moment she named a movie, the expression on his face told her she had picked the wrong one. "He said, 'No, we're not going to see that. We're going to this other movie.' But I had heard about that movie. It had violence and nudity, and it was just not my kind of show. So I told him I didn't want to see it. And, oh, it was terrible. He backhanded me right there in front of the movie theater. He hit me so hard I was sprawled on the sidewalk. There were so many people there who knew us, and they all just looked at me. And he goes, 'Well, get up. No one cares.' And he was right. No one did care. No one did anything…anything at all."

I imagine myself as a witness to Brad's attack, standing with my husband in front of that movie theater. I visualize the two of us helping Whitney up and offering to drive her home. This is what we would have done…I think. I hope. What, I ask Whitney, does she wish had happened that night? She thinks for a moment, replaying the scene. All she wanted, she finally says, was an acknowledgment of the episode. It would have been enough if someone had said "Hey, Brad, I saw that." When no one spoke, the silence was her answer. "So this is okay? This is fine? This happens to everybody, is that what they're trying to tell me? I was so confused…I sat in that movie theater thinking, no one else had a problem with that but me."

There were many other episodes. Now and then Whitney would break up with Brad. Weeks or months would pass with no contact between them. He was always in the background, though, and made sure she knew it. The triangle became his secret sign. "I don't know why he chose a triangle, but he used to leave things of mine in the shape of a triangle to let me know that he'd been there. Like he'd sneak into my house and he'd move my bed and my dresser and my couch into a triangle in the middle of my room. Or he'd do it with my damp clothes in the girl's locker room where, of course, men aren't allowed, so I'd know he was around somewhere, watching me."

Whitney's relationship with Brad followed the same pattern for three years. His abuse would reach intolerable limits. She would break up with him. He would eventually win her back with a combination of gifts, promises, and subtle threats. Then the cycle would repeat. It seemed to Whitney as though she would never find a way to break free. Until the day of her high school graduation. "I was standing in the backyard of his family's house in my swim suit. I was dripping wet and my face was blue, because one of his favorite tricks was to drag me into the pool and hold me under the water. Brad looked at me and said 'You know, you're never gonna be good enough.' And it's then that I realized: he's right. I'm not. I'm never going to be good enough for him, so why am I even trying? Because he's right, I never will measure up to what he wants. And then I thought, I'm glad! I'm glad I don't have to have big long hair and be a size nothing and disappear into space. I really don't want this."

That day Whitney broke up with Brad. Something in her tone of voice told him that this time she really meant it. The following weekend, he parked his BMW convertible on Whitney's street and watched the Benson house. When he was sure Whitney was alone, he entered the house through a basement window and raped her. This stark fact is all Whitney wants to tell me of what went on that afternoon, and all I need to know.

Except this. Two years later, seemingly innocuous sights can send Whitney into a state of panic. Triangles. BMWs. Country music. Even flowers. "Guys bring me flowers sometimes when they come to pick me up for a date and I'm just like, 'Oh, no!' Because to me flowers mean he's either going to do something bad to me, or he already has."

Except this. Whitney has nightmares. "Stupid things will trigger it. Brad always wore Eternity cologne. If I smell it, then that night I'll have a nightmare. I try to tell myself before I go to sleep, 'You're okay, think about something good, think about something good.' But then I'll have a dream and I'll wake up and realize it wasn't a dream, it was real, that really did happen to me." Whitney sought counseling, with the hope that therapy might help her sleep more peacefully. Though her instinct was correct, her choice of therapist was not. "She just wanted to know what had attracted me to Brad, and how he compared with my father. Then she talked a lot about how I can prevent this from happening to me again, and how I brought it on myself in the first place. I never went back to her. This was *him*. This was *Brad*. This was what *he* wanted, it wasn't what I wanted."

Except this. Though many of Whitney's friends are engaged, she has spent the past two years keeping men at a distance. "I'm so afraid to even date a person, let alone to get married and have kids. I'm just terrified of my honeymoon. I mean, I'll probably just plead with my husband...please let's not have a honeymoon. Let's just, you know, maybe hug each other every day and that will be plenty for me."

Whitney's scars are barely perceptible. Unless you knew they were there, you wouldn't see them. She does not look like a rape victim or a target of dating violence. She appears to be precisely what she is: a bright, sociable, energetic college student. She shares an apartment near campus with two girlfriends. She spent this summer working at a camp for handicapped children. She is considering switching her major to special education. In special education, she tells me, it doesn't matter what you look like. "The kids don't care about your dress size. They care about who you are and everything that you have to give." Whitney has a great deal to give. I am not convinced she knows it yet.

❧ Reflection ❧

Whitney's story raises some unique and troubling issues. She and Brad were not married; were not even living together. There were no children. There was no financial dependence. So why, why, why did she keep going back to him? To understand the reasons, you have to look beyond Whitney to her family, her school, her community. During the three years they dated, she never got the message that Brad was doing anything wrong. Friends at school took Brad's part and refused to believe Whitney's accusations. Brad's father silently watched him push her down the stairs. The town silently watched him knock her down at the movie theater. Her parents encouraged their romance. They accepted the convoluted excuses Brad invented to explain her scars. They never noticed her weight loss or his initials etched on her thighs. Given the degree of collusion that surrounded her, I don't find Whitney's behavior at all astonishing. In fact, I am amazed that she ever found the courage to break up with Brad. I am also impressed that she did not turn to any of the self-destructive behaviors that tempt today's teenagers. She finished high school, went on to college, and got on with her life. Scars and all.

Well, you may be thinking, this was a small Mormon town in the middle of nowhere. A town invested in maintaining the image of white-picket-fence America. Such a thing would never go on in our community. But it does. All the time. Brad's public attack at the movie theater mirrored a similar incident in my life. In the fall of 1972, travelling to spend Thanksgiving weekend with friends in Oregon, Melvin and I had a short layover in O'Hare Airport. It was the day before Thanksgiving; the terminal was thick with crowds. Sternly instructing me to wait right where I was, Melvin left to make a telephone call. I stood obediently for long minutes, trying not to think about my uncomfortably full bladder. Eventually, physiology got the better of me. I made a mad dash to the ladies room and an even madder dash back to my assigned place, but I was too late; Melvin had returned.

He was furious. He grabbed my wrist and began pulling me through the airport to our departure gate. As he pulled, he swore. As he swore, he slapped my face. We must have presented quite a sight to the other travelers. Yet nobody said a word. Nobody gave a sign that the sight of an angry man yanking a weeping woman through an airport was at all objectionable.

Three decades later and a thousand miles further west, Whitney got the same message I did. Yet, had either of us been attacked by a stranger, I have no doubt that some brave soul would have stepped forward.

Whitney's parents are an important part of her story. I am not a therapist; there may be family dynamics in the Benson household that have not occurred to me. I do not have children; there may be aspects of raising a teenager that explain what appears to be supreme neglect. I do, however, well remember what it was to be a teenager. I well remember the extent to which my parents hovered. They knew where I went, whom I saw, and (very nearly) all I did. Not that I did much — this was still the era when Good Girls didn't. But surely they, unlike Whitney's parents, would have noticed signs of abuse.

And yet. And yet. Shortly after Melvin and I married, my parents made the four-hour drive from New York to visit us in Boston. Several weeks earlier, he had slapped my face for the first time. I confided in my mother, pouring out the ugly details: the argument, the explosion, the slap, the tears. She was silent for a moment. Then came a rambling babble of words. Tension. Marital adjustment. Communication. Compromise. Hormones. I quickly dropped the subject. Obviously, Melvin had been right all along. This was my fault. I was provoking him.

Twenty-five years later my parents and I sit on the balcony of their winter condo. Though we rarely discuss my first marriage, we do so tonight, haltingly, our eyes fixed on the reds and golds of a Florida sunset. I should have come to them for help, my father says. I did, I reply. And I repeat the conversation. The sun has dropped behind the palm trees. Though I can barely see their faces, I feel the outlines of their dismay. My mother's voice is heavy with remorse: not only did she fail to protect me at the time, she has absolutely no memory of the incident. Hearing her stammered apology, any sense of betrayal I may have once felt evaporates. She loved me. She cared about me. Had she realized that I was being abused, she would have been fierce in her defense of me. But she literally did not hear me tell her that Melvin had slapped me. I understand. With no experience of abuse in her own marriage, my words that summer were as incomprehensible to my mother as if I had suddenly begun speaking Ancient Norse.

Whitney eventually did confide in her parents, though not until she broke up with Brad for the last time. Not until she had been raped. Their support was immediate and whole-hearted. Her father worked with the police to issue a restraining order against Brad. Her mother brought her to a therapist. Though they still don't know the full extent of Brad's abuse (and Whitney has no intention of burdening them with this information), what little they do know horrifies them. I wish they had been paying attention while it was going on. I wish they had noticed her distress, examined her wounds, rejected her excuses, confronted her, protected her. Perhaps she would be carrying fewer scars. I wish Whitney had confided in her parents, but I can fully appreciate why she chose not to. Like the mother of three who finally finds the courage to escape with her children to a battered women's shelter, Whitney was unable to ask for help from others until she had begun the process of helping herself.

It has been over a year since I interviewed Whitney. We swap postcards occasionally. This summer she sent me a college graduation announcement. I sent her a present. Unlike the other stories in this book, I don't know how Whitney's will turn out. I worry about her. She has been deeply traumatized; I am not sure she realizes how deeply.

From my perspective of thirty years, as well as a loving second marriage to a warm and caring man, I find it unbearably sad that Whitney's first sexual experience was a rape. I am sure she believes — as who would not? — that all future sexual encounters will be more or less the same. No wonder she dreads her wedding night. I suspect that counseling would help Whitney, if she were lucky enough to find the right thera-pist. Unfortunately, the therapist she consulted spent the session probing Whitney's attachment to her father, her neu-rotic neediness, and her secret desire to be hurt. Whitney never returned for a second helping. Good for her, I say. Yet how will she heal on her own?

After her experience at the television station, Whitney consulted a plastic surgeon. Yes, she was told, dermabra-sion could probably minimize their appearance, but the scars would never vanish completely. Whitney worries about the scars on her body; I worry about the scars on her soul. Over time, she may accept that her scars are as much a part of her as her brown eyes and her effervescent personality.

I hope she does. But I am furious that she has to.

8
Andrea Hartley

Was It My Fault?

It honestly amazes me that I'm 47 years old, I have by
any kind of standards achieved success in the world, I
must be pretty intelligent to have become a doctor. I am
not a superstitious person. I am not in any way that I
can see an irrational person. And yet I can still sit here
and say out loud that I was convinced then, in some
ways I still believe, that he could read my mind.

I am seated at a conference table with a group of third-
year medical students, conducting a workshop entitled
"Domestic Violence: Myth and Reality." The human mind cannot hold what it cannot grasp, I explain, and so we humans
invent mental models. Mental models are our way of making
sense of the world. It is inconceivable that a strong woman
can also be a battered woman. The two would seem to be
mutually exclusive. Consequently, I continue, warming to my
topic, we create an image of a battered woman that makes
more sense. We presume she is a weak, uneducated person
with low self-esteem who marries young and produces six
children in seven years. She marries a batterer because her
father beat her mother; this is all she knows of marriage. She
remains with him because she has nowhere else to go, no job
skills, no means to support her children.

The medical students nod wisely: this model of domestic violence nicely matches theirs. Then I tell them about Dr. Andrea Hartley. She married when she was thirty. The beatings began on their honeymoon.

Unfortunately, Andrea's story does not have the impact I had intended. I wanted the students to realize that mental models are often faulty. I hoped that, as future doctors, the story of a doctor who was also a battered woman would force them to examine their own mental models of domestic violence, snapping them apart like Lego blocks, discarding the bits they would now see as false stereotypes. Instead, a hand goes up, and a medical student at the other end of the conference table clearly and confidently presents his diagnosis. Eureka! Andrea was thirty and unmarried? Then she must have been desperate — willing to marry even an abusive man rather than face the prospect of being single for the rest of her life! Another mental model; another attempt to hammer an oddly-shaped block into place rather than tear down the structure and begin again.

I cannot blame the medical students for questioning Andrea's judgment. She questions it herself. "I think there certainly were signs before I actually married him," she tells me. "There were many signs, and it was kind of like an interlocking chain. If I believed one aspect, if I believed one piece was really wrong, then I would have had to see all the other pieces. And it was not possible or simply not a choice I made at the time to examine it."

Andrea is forty-seven, a Seattle pediatrician with a thriving private practice. Her abusive marriage occupies only the tiniest corner of her history: she left seventeen years ago, after only four months of marriage. Everyone asks why battered women don't just leave their batterer. Andrea did. She left quickly, and she left completely. Gone. Goodbye. Yet still she wonders: why did she fall in love with Gregg? How was it that an intelligent, well-educated woman could have made such a bad decision? Perhaps, she reflects, her childhood was to blame. Not because she witnessed abuse growing up, but because she didn't. "I think part of it had to do with my own confusion, having never been in a relationship where I'd been threatened emotionally or physically. I came from an extremely loving family, where physical brutality or the threat of it was absolutely unheard of." I understand Andrea's need to find a rational explanation for what happened to her. I also see the irony in her analysis. The common assumption is that battered women come from violent childhoods: with violence as their norm, they don't think to protect themselves. Andrea, though, blames her peaceful childhood for her naïveté: with tranquility as her norm, she didn't know how to protect herself.

When Andrea began dating Gregg, she was in her third and final year of residency training at the Mayo Clinic. Residents are an overworked, underpaid, sleep-deprived lot; it was not unusual for Andrea to arrive at her apartment after forty-eight hours on call, too dirty to get into bed, too exhausted to shower, with just enough energy to strip off her hospital scrubs, struggle into a bathrobe, curl up on the bathroom rug and fall asleep. It doesn't take much to make a medical resident happy. A clean apartment. A hot meal. A silent telephone. A good night's sleep. Married residents barely see their spouses and children. Unmarried residents have a social life that falls somewhere on the continuum between negligible and nonexistent. It was in this context that Andrea Hartley met Gregg Ivers. She was flying back to Minnesota from one of her rare visits home to see her parents in Pittsburgh. The attractive man in the seat beside hers started a conversation. By the time the plane landed, he had asked her to have dinner with him, and she had accepted.

Within a month, Andrea was spending every minute of her limited free time with Gregg. They seemed to have a great deal in common. They both loved the theater. They both enjoyed long bike rides. They giggled at the same silly jokes. Best of all, Gregg was not a physician. Andrea had dated her share of doctors and concluded that she was not about to marry one. Much as she loved medicine, she didn't want to be surrounded by it twenty-four hours a day. Gregg was a stockbroker. He was charming, clever, and funny. All her friends said so. And she agreed. He certainly wasn't violent. He doted on her. He made her feel cherished. "I was very touched by the fact that he would call me at work to see how I was doing, because I worked sixty or seventy hours every week at the hospital. I thought it was really lovely that he called me at work. I thought it was lovely that he wanted to know about the people I worked with, about my friends, and he really listened to my long accounts."

In retrospect, Andrea frames Gregg's behavior in a different light. "Looking back now, I realize it was, in a sense, evidence gathering. It was a matter of having control, knowing where I was, knowing what my activities were." Andrea is almost apologetic as she ticks off the signs she should have seen, the behaviors she should have suspected. Yet I suspect it would have been nearly impossible to spot Gregg as the batterer he later became. He called her at work. He asked her about her day. He listened to her stories about her friends, her relatives, her colleagues, her patients. So what? This is what all newly smitten men do. It's called courtship. It doesn't last. Which is why Dear Abby and Ann Landers get so many letters from annoyed women about the attention their husbands lavish on their car (or their golf game, or their computer, or their bowling league, or their favorite sports team).

Andrea and Gregg dated for a year before they married. She was thirty, he was thirty-six. And on their honeymoon, this charming, clever, funny man turned into someone she didn't recognize. "Impossible," you may be thinking. "People don't change overnight." But batterers often do, and Gregg did. They were in Hawaii — where, incidentally, Andrea has flatly declared she will never again step foot. It is something of a family joke that she even refuses to eat Macadamia nuts. They were sitting across from each other in an elegant restaurant, sipping their coffee and sharing a dessert. She remembers every detail: the smell of Plumeria flowers, the red blaze of the sunset, the gentle splash of waves on nearby rocks. They weren't fighting; they weren't even talking. Without warning, Gregg picked up his cup of coffee and, with a quick flick of his wrist, sent the scalding liquid flying across the table. "I remember seeing this hot coffee coming at me. And I was wearing, because I was young and thin at the time, one of those little strapless sundress things. I remember feeling the hot coffee splash on my chest and Gregg saying, 'Oh my God, Andrea...how did you spill that on you, are you all right?' And I thought I was crazy. I really thought I was crazy."

This was the first of many incidents. The pattern never varied. There would be a violent outburst, seemingly out of the blue. Then there would be apologies, remorse, contrition. She would forgive him, because she couldn't allow herself to believe what was happening, because she was his wife, because as the weeks passed it became increasingly clear that he needed help, because she was in a helping profession. After each episode, despite his tears, despite his promises, he would have managed to subtly convey that she was to blame: that she had pushed his buttons until he had no choice but to explode. Andrea has trouble articulating what those weeks with Gregg were like. "Crazy" is the word she uses, again and again, to describe his actions, to describe her response, to describe the mastery that Gregg had gained over her thoughts and her feelings. "It honestly amazes me that I'm forty-seven years old, I have by any kind of standards achieved success in the world, I must be pretty intelligent to have become a doctor. I am not a superstitious person. I am not in any way that I can see an irrational person. And yet I can still sit here and say out loud that I was convinced then — in some ways I still believe — that he could read my mind."

The first time there is violence, Andrea reflects, we don't believe it. Next, we explain it away. Then we do whatever we can to cope. With no prior experience of abuse, no way to make sense of what was happening to her, Andrea coped by putting herself into a state of suspended animation. She still went to work at the hospital every day. She still looked at tonsils, stitched wounds, wrote prescriptions, and made careful notes in medical charts. But she felt nothing. She deliberately made herself numb. "There was no way to think about what was happening, so I decided not to think. And I didn't. For four months, I was just numb." And then Gregg did something that woke her up, galvanizing her into action. He forged a check from a bank account that her father had set up years ago for Andrea and her two sisters. "All I can tell you is, that was his big mistake." Beating her with enough commotion that neighbors called the police was one thing. Stealing from her family was quite another. The day Andrea discovered the forgery was the day she called her father. Gregg had beaten her up, she announced. She needed help. "My father came and got me. I was absolutely rescued by my family. They were incredible...wonderful. Actually, my biggest concern during that whole time was that my father was going to end up in jail! That he'd kill Gregg for what he had done to me."

Fortunately, Andrea's father managed to keep himself under control. A successful businessman, he called his law firm and set the wheels in motion for Andrea's divorce. That was when Andrea discovered an important fact that Gregg had taken great pains to conceal: she was his sixth wife. Her father also bought her a new car to replace the one that Gregg had convinced her to put in his name "for insurance purposes." His greatest help, though, was not financial but emotional. When she had been ready to escape, he had been there for her. No questions, no reprimands, nothing but unconditional support. Her colleagues at the hospital were equally supportive. "I felt very protected. I just felt so safe again."

Andrea acknowledges that she is much luckier than many other battered women: she had no children, no financial ties to her ex-husband, no difficult legal entanglements. Most women cannot walk away as easily as she did. She had the luxury of simply turning the page and beginning again. Still, she was much warier than she had been before her marriage. "I felt much more mistrustful, not surprisingly, after the divorce. I went out on a lot of first dates. I didn't especially feel like going out with anyone a second time. And then about six months after I left, I met Henry. And I went out with him on a second date because there was no doubt in my mind that he would never hit somebody. When I think back on it now, I can hardly believe it, but it's true: my initial relationship with Henry was based on my lack of fear rather than anything else. We've been married for fifteen years, and we have a very happy marriage, but I must say that's a pretty stupid reason for marrying somebody!"

After she finished her residency training, Andrea went into private practice in Minneapolis, joining an existing group of pediatricians. A compassionate and capable physician, she was soon carrying a full patient load. Seven years later, Henry received a tempting job offer from a large Seattle law firm. He broached the possibility of relocation hesitantly. Would she consider leaving Minneapolis and starting over again in another city? What surprised her was how readily she agreed. She wrote a letter to her 2,000 patients, sold her share of the practice, and moved to the Pacific Northwest with no professional contacts. "About a year later I was thinking about how it was so nice to be in Seattle and walk into a store, or a restaurant, or a theater, and not look around before I moved any further from the front door. And it was only then that it dawned on me why I had been so happy to leave Minnesota, where I'd lived for so many years, where my whole personal and professional life was based. Because now I could stop looking over my shoulder."

Andrea has become active in child abuse prevention. She frequently uses her authority as a pediatrician to advocate for funding and legislative reform. Several years ago she and a colleague conducted a one-day training program on domestic violence and child abuse for the medical staff at a nearby hospital. As they walked across the parking lot together, Andrea's colleague reflected on how difficult it is to teach doctors about family violence. After all, she continued, professional, well-educated people might be familiar with the statistics and mechanisms of battering, but since they have no personal experience, they cannot possibly appreciate what a violent relationship is really like. "People like us," she concluded, "wouldn't believe this could ever happen." Andrea took her time before replying, "Well, guess what, Marsha, it happened to me." There was a moment of silence. She could see Marsha's wheels spinning. "Out came the whole list of stereotypes: 'You're so articulate, Andrea. You're so smart, so sure of yourself. How could you?' I'm sure she didn't mean it to be hurtful, but her response was so typical. I could see that she blamed me for allowing it to happen."

Andrea, for the most part, has stopped blaming herself. "For a long time I was so ashamed that I could be so stupid…as though this has anything to do with stupidity. How could it happen to a doctor? As though being a doctor has anything to do with it! If it could happen to me, it could happen to anyone. Nobody, including myself, goes into a relationship because they want to be hurt. They go into a relationship for the same reason everybody else does."

❧ Reflection ❧

On April 20, 1999, in Littleton, Colorado, two students murdered a teacher and twelve of their classmates at Columbine High School. By the next morning, journalists and talk show panelists were grappling with the question: what was it about the upbringing of these two boys that caused them to commit such an act? Everyone needed to feel that this could not possibly happen in their community, in their family. We examined the boys' parents under the lens of a high-powered microscope. We looked for clues: some mistake they made that we wouldn't have made, some flaw in them that we don't share, so that we could believe that their tragedy would never be ours. We attempted to find an explanation, but ultimately there was no explanation. There was no one to blame. That is what makes tragedies tragic: we cannot protect ourselves from them. If history teaches nothing else, it teaches that great good can come out of achingly desperate circumstances, while great evil can flourish in the midst of privilege.

When I speak to groups about domestic abuse, audience members ask far more questions about the battered women than about the men who batter them. Were these women raised in violent homes? Did they suffer from low self-esteem? Did they abuse drugs or alcohol? Did they escape from one abuser, only to run to another? There was a time when these questions, with their unstated implication that an abused woman is to blame for her own abuse, set my teeth on edge. Anything to question the victim rather than the perpetrator, I used to inwardly rage. Anything to make an abused woman the author of her own abuse: too young or too old, too rich or too poor, too sheltered or too seasoned.

I am no longer angry when I hear these questions; I have come to understand their purpose. The message I deliver when I teach and write about domestic violence is that there is no "typical" battered woman. Any girl or woman might be battered. This is a message no one wants to hear: the thought that we are safe only by random chance or good fortune makes people acutely uncomfortable. Like the Columbine High School shootings, people need to separate themselves from the possibility of domestic violence in their own lives. And so they look for ways in which they are different from these women. If there is something wrong with her, then I am safe. If she came from a broken home, I am safe because my childhood was stable. If she drinks like a fish, I am safe because I merely sip an occasional glass of Chardonnay. If she worships at a particular church, I am safe because I attend the one down the road. If she married at twenty, I am safe because I intend to wait until I'm thirty. If, as in Andrea's case, she married at thirty, then…well…it serves her right for waiting too long.

Blaming an abused woman for her own abuse, people feel safe from similar abuse. Ironically, nobody does a better job of blaming the victims than the victims themselves. Andrea still questions her judgment in choosing Gregg. She still believes, deep in her heart, that his actions say something about her.

People get itchy when I say that any woman might fall prey to domestic violence. They practically break out in hives when I follow that statement with this one: it is extraordinarily difficult to spot a batterer in advance. I'm sorry — I wish it were easy. I wish I could post a checklist of warning signs; a set of criteria that would allow a woman to diagnose a batterer during the early stages of courtship, when she can extricate herself with relative ease. Professional women in their mid to late twenties are typically the ones who clamor for such a list. They are, of course, asking for themselves. They look at me, seeing their mothers, seeing an older version of themselves. I am disconcertingly like them: educated, articulate, poised. Privileged. Yet I married an abuser. What red flags did I miss, they ask me, that they can watch out for? There were none, I reply, accurately predicting their looks of skepticism. But it's true. During the courtship period, most batterers look just like every other man in love. They demonstrate only kind, nurturing, attentive behavior. Women are drawn to men who listen to them, and batterers get it just right. When Andrea and Gregg were dating, if she was scheduled to make a presentation at a national pediatrics meeting, he would call her hotel room the previous night to ask how she was feeling. He would call early the next morning to be sure she hadn't overslept, and to reassure her that the lecture would be a smashing success. Once they married, Gregg's attention turned to intrusion. He would call her hotel room, not to reassure her, but to reassure himself…that she was there, that she was alone, that she belonged to him.

The difficulty is that courtship always puts two people on their best behavior. Until the courtship period is over, it is very nearly impossible to correctly interpret that behavior. A man gives his sweetheart an expensive piece of jewelry. Is this a loving gesture, or a manipulative ploy to make her feel obligated to him? He calls her every night to see how her day went. Is he honestly interested, or is he checking up on her? He compliments her dress, her hair, her nail polish. Is he simply a man in the first throes of romance (my husband of twenty-some years loves me dearly, but he hasn't the faintest idea what I was wearing when I left the house this morning; for all he knows, I could have been dressed in pajamas and bunny slippers), or is he establishing a pattern of control?

When does attentiveness cross the threshold into possessive jealousy? When does supportiveness become control? How much interest is too much interest? "Head tennis," my friend Wendy calls this, as the competing interpretations bat themselves from one side of the mental net to the other.

Andrea blames herself because she didn't see the threat that lurked behind Gregg's loving courtship. Without a crystal ball, no one could have seen it.

9
Dawn Kincaid

Am I Really Safe?

*My work was my protection. Building the company was
so important, I wasn't about to let a real relationship in
because it would interfere with my survival and my
livelihood. I needed to feel safe. That was predominant.
I thought, okay, I'm on my own, nobody's going to take
care of me, I've got to do whatever it takes to make this
company successful.*

Dawn Kincaid had a horror of a childhood. She never knew
her birth parents. Her adoptive father, a man she calls "an
alcoholic and a scary man to all of us," sexually molested her
from the time she was a toddler until she left home to attend
Oregon State College. Her adoptive mother chose not to see
what she felt powerless to stop. Dawn had a group of girlfriends when she was in grade school, but kept very much to
herself throughout high school and college.

By the time she met Randy Falvo, she had put her ugly
and painful childhood firmly behind her. After graduating from
college in 1967, with a double major in business administration and psychology, she moved to Portland and took a job
with what was, at the time, the country's only telephone company. She was pleased to be financially independent, earning
a respectable salary as a first-level manager in the data pro-

cessing department. These were the days when computers were enormous, finicky beasts tended by the Elect Few. A computer generally had its own room. Bell Telephone's computer had its own cluster of low brick buildings.

Randy was Dawn's first serious boyfriend. Working twenty hours a week while attending college had left her little time for a social life. Randy, who had graduated from college six years earlier, was two levels further up Bell Telephone's rigid organizational hierarchy. He was from Montana, the only son of a prominent ranching family. He was bright, articulate, and something of a cowboy. He drank heavily. He ran with a crowd that experimented with marijuana, mescaline, and LSD. The drugs and alcohol seemed in keeping with the rest of his personality. In fact, the more he drank, the more lucid and charming he became. Being high never seemed to interfere with his work performance. Dawn, raised by an alcoholic father, did not see Randy's drinking as an obstacle. It was, if not precisely pleasant, at least familiar.

Many abusers are difficult to spot in advance. Randy Falvo was abusive from the beginning. "He didn't change substantially until the end, when I was pregnant and he was violent physically. But he was always emotionally and verbally nasty. He was just amazing with language — he had a real facility. He had studied law, though he hadn't taken the bar. He was one of the most cutting people I've ever encountered: extraordinarily cruel with words. I just wrote it off. There was a dear part of him, but there was also this other part which was really an angry, drug- and alcohol-abusing man." Were she to meet a man like Randy now, Dawn insists, she would never allow him into her life. She believes the pattern of her childhood virtually assured that she would be drawn to such a cruel man. "When I think about where I came from, and the abuse that was in my family of origin, this marriage was actually better than the home that I had left."

Many abusers carry out their attacks in secret, presenting an image to the world that differs substantially from the one their family sees. Randy never tried to hide his snide remarks and caustic insults. He was more abusive in public, Dawn recalls, than he was when they were alone. I find that interesting, and tell her so. My experience has been that most women report the opposite. Dawn thinks a moment, then revises her statement. "I guess it just hurt more when it was public. I guess my point is, now that I'm saying it and realizing, that he didn't bother to censor himself. It wasn't anything he felt he needed to hide."

Dawn and Randy lived together for two years. They were married in the fall of 1969. By this time, Dawn had been promoted to a second-level management position, with increased responsibility, autonomy, and salary. Randy, however, had turned into rather a failure. Promotion after promotion passed him by, as senior managers took note of his increasingly hungover mornings and late lunches. "He was so unhappy with his life," Dawn says. "He was such a bright man, yet he hadn't found his place. So when his father wanted him to come back to the business, Randy jumped at the chance." In April of 1970, Randy suddenly announced that they were going home. Home, to Randy, was Bozeman, Montana. His father wanted him to learn ranching: the business he would, as the only son, ultimately inherit. And what, asked Dawn indignantly, was she supposed to do with herself in Bozeman? What about her career? Did Montana even have phone lines? Or were they still using the Pony Express?

Nevertheless, Randy was firm. There was big money to be made in ranching, and he wanted his share. Within a month they were living in the house Randy's parents had purchased for them in Bozeman. Montana turned out to be significantly less remote than Dawn had feared. Tumbleweeds did not roll through the downtown streets. Inhabitants enjoyed all the modern conveniences: electricity, indoor plumbing, and telephones. Her strong performance rating at Bell Telephone helped her land a comparable management position at the company's Bozeman office. The director of the data processing department was happy to have such a professional, competent, hardworking employee. If, however, Dawn had harbored a secret hope that the clean Montana air would somehow cure Randy's drinking and cruelty, she was disappointed. Their marriage continued along the same path it had been on from the beginning. Randy continued to drink. He continued to use drugs. Since Dawn never knew when he would arrive home drunk, stoned, and raging, she had to maintain a constant state of vigilance. "I just never knew when my husband was going to blow, or when I was going to come home and he would have been home drinking all day, or when he was going to go out with friends and do drugs. I had a career, but he was really my full-time job."

Dawn enumerates the factors that kept her from leaving Randy. "Here I was in the middle of Montana. My husband's family was enormously wealthy: they basically owned the town. The ranching community was so connected and so closed that I was very much an outsider. I just worked and I was a wife. I developed no personal friendships…I don't think I had a single woman friend. I had no support. And I took seriously my marriage vows. So, really, I didn't even think about getting out. I assumed this was what I had to do. This was the way it was." It never occurred to her that this wasn't necessarily the way it had to be. She had never seen a marriage that contradicted her assumption. Certainly not when she was growing up. And Randy's family was not much better. "His dad was terribly mean to his mother. And his mother was an alcoholic. So, with them as my model, it wasn't any worse than what was happening to me. And, finally, I believed that he truly did love me."

She was also afraid of what Randy might do if she left. Not what he'd do to her, but what he'd do to himself. She worried that his drinking would get out of control. She also worried that he would make good on his threat to commit suicide. "I think it would have been largely a pride or a possession issue. Saving face." Indeed. How could Randy hold his head up in this small town, the town his family virtually owned, if his wife left him?

At Dawn's insistence, they went to their pastor for counseling. But she had no words to describe what was wrong with her marriage. "Domestic violence" and "verbal abuse" were not the common terms they are today. All she could report was a vague sense of unease. She was unhappy. She felt unfulfilled. She did not enjoy their sexual relations. "So we had a few marriage counseling sessions, but it was all show. That was the family church. That was the family pastor. Do you think he was going to say anything?" Frustrated with the pastor's soothing platitudes, Dawn suggested therapy. But Randy was just as nasty to the therapist as he was to Dawn. "He was horrible. Just horrible! I had never seen him so nasty to any human being." After a few sessions, the outraged therapist threw Randy out of his office. He agreed to continue seeing Dawn, and she took him up on the offer. Though she found their sessions useful, she was unable to discuss the central issues that lurked beneath the surface of her life. Her father's sexual abuse. Her husband's drinking. She kept thinking there was something wrong with her. She kept trying to fix herself.

Dawn had turned to a pastor and a psychologist for help. Now she turned to a lover. On a business trip, she met a man who was her counterpart in Bell Telephone's Albuquerque office. Their affair lasted for nearly a year. "All that really was," Dawn says with a touch of embarrassment, "was an angry statement." They didn't see each other often. He was married. So was she. It was difficult to arrange their professional and personal lives to accommodate more than a few long weekends together. But Dawn clung to their infrequent meetings the way a struggling fifth grader clings to the image of summer vacation. When Randy was especially drunk or particularly vicious, she would think about her lover, wrapping their secret around herself, blunting the edge of Randy's knife-like words. So when the man abruptly broke off their affair, she felt hurt, betrayed, and alone. "In some ways, I loved him more than my husband. Part of me believed he would help me escape, and he didn't. In the end, I had to turn to myself for that."

It was shortly after the affair ended that Dawn became pregnant. The act that led to conception was a rape. There is no other word for it, though in those days no one believed that a rape could occur within the confines of marriage. Nevertheless, that was what it was: a husband arriving home drunk in the middle of the night, forcing himself on his unwilling wife. "There was so little support about what was happening to me! It was a typical first trimester: I was very tired. I wasn't really throwing up very much, but I had just enormous fatigue, and I was diligently working full-time. Also, it was summertime, and brutally hot." Randy became increasingly upset at Dawn's tiredness, at her lack of attentiveness to his needs. "I was focussed on myself for a change, and on the baby. I don't know how I raised his ire enough, but at one point he hit me. Hard. And that was the end."

That weekend, Randy's college roommate was coming to stay and Randy had planned a large party in his honor. Dawn remembers the heat. She remembers long hours in the kitchen preparing canapés. Between the temperature, the exhaustion, and the memory of Randy's physical attack, Dawn miscarried on Sunday night. Her primary feeling was relief. "I knew that I had my freedom. Had I had that child, I would have been facing for a lifetime the marriage that his parents had. And I could see it with such clarity. I could see that Randy and I would wind up like that." She told Randy that the marriage was over. He pleaded. He begged. But Dawn was not to be moved. He moved out of their house, she changed the locks, and their divorce was final in six months.

Dawn's voice softens as she tells me what happened to Randy. He stood up to his father, declaring that he wasn't interested in ranching, that he was going to take the bar exam and practice law. To everyone's surprise, he became a successful and extremely wealthy lawyer. "It was a gift," Dawn concludes serenely, putting her bad memories to rest. "It was actually my gift to him. Not that he ever resolved all the issues that had made him the way he was. I hate to think about what his father had done to him. So I can't say that he lived a happy life. But in terms of my leaving him, I really gave him a chance, and it worked for him. Isn't that nice?" Randy died ten years ago. Dawn was sorry to hear it. He was the way he was for many reasons; she just feels fortunate to have been given a way out.

Dawn continued working at Bell Telephone for a year. Then

she got a new boss: a man who didn't like women, didn't believe they should be promoted to positions of authority, and certainly didn't believe they had any place in the data processing end of the business. She could see that she was being bypassed. "I watched men making more money than me, and male management trainees coming in to take management positions that I had been in line for. In hindsight, I see that I was just so angry! Here I finally had made my stand, gotten out of my abusive marriage, and now I was getting similar abuse at work." It was clear to Dawn that she was going to have to transfer to a different location. But then she sat back and thought about it. Why, after all, should she leave? She had developed a network of women friends. She was active in the arts (Bozeman, a college town, has more of a cultural life than you might think). She was seeing a therapist whom she really trusted. She liked her house. She was just beginning to feel grounded, just beginning to feel strong. Why should she slink away, a victim of an obnoxious boss, and leave behind the new life she was just beginning to enjoy? "I was uprooted every other year as a kid, moving from town to town as my dad lost jobs and found jobs. So there was part of me that really wanted to just stay where I was rooted. I was connected with the arts, I was connected politically, and I was building my own community for the first time in my life."

From a position of strength, she decided to form her own consulting company, providing computer systems to handle the expanding data processing needs of the rapidly-growing telecommunications industry. DataSource Group, she called it, taking the initials from her maiden name, which she had reclaimed the moment her divorce became final. Dawn S. Grant. DSG. Steel-gray letters embossed on thick white linen paper; her business stationery spoke to her clarity, her professionalism, her determination to succeed. Her first consulting jobs were small. She struggled for two years to gain recognition and credibility. Eventually, her hard work and long hours paid off. By the time I met Dawn, DSG had a strong client base and an excellent reputation throughout the telecommunications industry.

It was easy for Dawn to dedicate herself to her new role as an entrepreneur. She lived a rather glamorous life. On Thursday she might fly to New York to see a client. She would remain in Manhattan for the weekend, attending a play, a concert, and a few art gallery openings. On Monday morning, she would be on a plane to Chicago. "I was successful enough that I could afford to fly around the country, go to these wonderful places, stay in nice, quaint, small hotels, and live a jet-setter life. I would be walking in to make sales calls on senior vice-presidents, and I made sure I looked the part. I certainly wasn't opposed to it; I thought it was a lot of fun!"

I met Dawn in the summer of 1977, five years after she formed DSG, eighteen months after I left Melvin. We were on the same project team for a large computer system design effort. We were both consultants, but we did not carry equal weight on the project. She was important: the president of a million-dollar consulting firm. I was small fry. She was my role model; my vision of what a successful consultant ought to be. We remained in touch. With the 1984 deregulation of the communications industry and the proliferation of personal computers, technology was a hot field for consultants. Occasionally the same company that hired DSG to design their data processing system would hire me to write the user guides and develop the training program that explained how the system worked. Dawn was, I knew, divorced. But we never discussed our ex-husbands. Had we done so, we would have learned that we had more in common than Frequent Flyer miles and a weakness for Ferragamo shoes. But both of us had put that part of our lives firmly behind us. Both of us had professional images to maintain. A victim of domestic violence, a person who had allowed herself to be beaten and belittled, was not an image we would have wanted the world to associate with either of us.

Dawn was an aggressive entrepreneur. The more prominent she became, the safer she felt. "My work was my protection. Building the company was so important, I wasn't about to let a real relationship in because it would interfere with my survival and my livelihood. I needed to feel safe. That was predominant. I thought, okay, I'm on my own, nobody's going to take care of me, I've got to do whatever it takes to make this company successful. I was out making sales calls and it was up to me, and my behavior, to understand how to meet the needs of my clients. Building my business helped me get functional, because that feedback from my sales calls was perfect. If I didn't do it right, if my anger showed through, if I didn't take responsibility, I couldn't be successful enough to survive this business."

Dawn and I go back more than twenty years. Even so, I pose my next question tentatively. Does it strike her as noteworthy, I ask, that she chose an industry with such a predictable link between cause and effect? Computers are dependable. They can be controlled. What you put in is what you get out. Cause and effect: the key element that was missing in her childhood and her marriage. "I clung to it," she replies instantly, her voice suddenly thick with emotion. "Oh, dear...I can feel the tears. That's why the business was so important. It allowed me to live in a rational world, and I'd never known that. It was all rational, you know, it all made sense. So much of what I was doing with DSG was bringing this clarity and this rationality to a world that had always felt like chaos."

While Dawn was jet setting around the country, wearing St. John knit suits, staying at boutique hotels, and increasing DSG's sales figures, her personal life was less impressive. She dated, of course. She had a few affairs. But she always found herself choosing men that were, in some way, unsuitable. She took pride in her self-reliance. "It was an extension of my childhood — I see that now, though I couldn't see it then. I had a mother who didn't mother me, I had a father who was always accosting me, and I had been groomed by those two to be self-sufficient. Because I was adopted, they made it clear that I had to be grateful. That it was my job to make them proud. I had to earn my keep. So after the divorce, all of my normal instincts were to make a life for myself alone."

The business gave her the perfect excuse for avoiding intimacy. The longer she was involved with DSG, the less able she was to imagine herself back in corporate life. Her autonomy was too important to her. "There was a huge drive to make the business work, and I wasn't about to let a real relationship in because it would interfere with my survival and my livelihood." For eleven years, Dawn's life revolved around her work. "And I remember that I reached a point where it just got old. I didn't have a soulmate, I didn't have somebody that I got to cuddle up and sleep with at night."

Dawn believes that her change of heart had a lot to do with finally feeling on firm financial ground. "I felt safe enough that my business was doing well, that it was going to survive.

It was no longer a surprise that I got more sales every year. The systems I developed were receiving rave reviews. I had staff, I had impressive sales, I had huge financial success. And I remember saying to a close woman friend, 'I think I'm ready for some balance in my life.' And by that I meant, it wouldn't be a married man this time. I wanted the real thing. I wanted to have a real relationship."

That weekend she flew to Kansas City, where she had been invited to deliver the keynote address at a conference for software developers. And in the elevator, on her way downstairs to the speakers' cocktail party, she met Tom Kincaid. "It was love at first sight," she says softly, the hard business edge melting out of her voice. "Not that I trusted that feeling," she quickly amends. Tom was a senior vice president at Lincoln National Life Insurance. He was based in Fort Wayne, Indiana — a hefty trip from Bozeman, requiring two plane changes in each direction. But within a year, Dawn was making the commute every weekend. When Tom was offered a position with an insurance firm in Kansas City, he asked Dawn if she would consider moving both herself and the DSG offices. "The timing was right. So I picked up and moved. But we lived together for three years...I actually wasn't all that eager to get married."

Tom kept urging Dawn to marry him, and she kept refusing. "I went into this marriage kicking and screaming, but I'm so glad that we did it. It was a step up in a level of commitment." Dawn only realized this after their wedding; she believed she had been totally committed to him while they were living together. She had envisioned them being together forever. "But I hadn't been willing to make that next step. I felt, why ruin a perfectly lovely relationship?"

Tom and Dawn have been married for eleven years. But it

would be doing a disservice to Dawn to end her story with her marriage, as though all she needed to achieve happiness was the love of a good man. Victims of child abuse carry their demons with them. Three years after she married Tom, Dawn realized that she needed to go back into therapy. She couldn't put her finger on anything specific. But she felt strongly that there was something wrong with her life. "I knew I wasn't living joyously. This was despite the fact that I had a great husband, I owned a successful company…on the surface, it all looked idyllic. Yet there was just something not working, and I couldn't figure out what it was. Everything looked so perfect…yet I wanted more."

In therapy for the second time, Dawn finally realized that she had never come to terms with the abuse in her life, the abuse that reached deep into her past, well before her first marriage. "I had to go back to my roots. I had to go back and revisit my adoption — because not only did I have the sexual abuse, but I also had the issue of not being wanted, of being given up at birth." Patiently, over a period of years, with the help of a competent and compassionate therapist, she uncovered the issues of trust and fear that she had carried with her into her second marriage. "My first round of therapy twenty years ago got me functional enough to do great things in the business world, but I needed help to understand how to do relationships. That was this next round."

Dawn credits her marriage to Tom for bringing her to the point where she was willing to relive the pain of her childhood. "I was fine when I didn't have to make the commitment, when we were just living together. When I didn't feel safe, I had escape routes: I could just hop on an airplane and go make a sales call. But once I was married and it required a real level of commitment, I knew that I needed more help to be able to do that." Dawn is convinced that she and Tom would not be where they are today, had she not received that help. "I bet we'd still be married," she muses, "but we sure wouldn't be in the bliss that we're in."

Dawn sees her life as a journey towards truth. An impressive objective for someone who spent her childhood surrounded by betrayal and deceit. "When I stood for the truth," she concludes, her voice vibrant, "we all won. I got to build my business, my ex-husband got to create the success that he needed, and my clients were helped. It was good all around...there wasn't a down side anywhere. And by the time I got healthy enough, I actually got to meet the man of my dreams."

🎋 Reflection 🎋

That there are stories such as Dawn's should not be surprising. People do, after all, survive astonishing adversity. Survive, and grow, and even laugh. Every woman in an abusive relationship, whether she leaves or not, is a survivor. Dawn's childhood made her a survivor long before she met Randy. Survival: existence in spite of adversity. In spite of the daily assaults on character and dignity, women continue to exist — even, like Dawn, to move beyond stagnant existence to impressive growth.

Survival is never easy. Like every prisoner of war, I am not proud of some of the things I did to survive. Here is one. The middle years of my marriage to Melvin were marked by the clash between my deep desire for a child and my husband's terror of fatherhood. Not that he framed it that way; I would, he insisted, make a terrible mother. I was too selfish. Too immature. Projection, I believe this is called: the attribution of one's own attitudes, feelings, and ideas to another as a defense against anxiety. (In retrospect, denying me a child may have been Melvin's one act of generosity. Dawn's experience is sadly common. A child, even a pregnancy, tends to exacerbate the violence of abusive men. At the time, though, his refusal to allow me to become pregnant seemed his worst act of cruelty.)

During this time, Melvin was attending law school and I was teaching third grade. At an end-of-finals party for the second year law students, I conversed with the mother-in-law of one. She told me how thrilled she was with her one-year-old grandson, born just before her son-in-law's Constitutional Law exam. She chuckled at the memory. "Maybe with an entrance like that, this little boy will be on the Supreme Court some day!" She went on at some length about how much her daughter enjoyed Motherhood. Mindful of my husband's hovering presence, I subdued my natural inclination to participate in this woman's delight. Had I been at the party alone, I would have made satisfying cooing noises over the baby pictures that made a happy bulge in this proud grandmother's purse. Instead, I asked, "What does your daughter do?" To which her mother replied, with a certain degree of huff, "She takes care of a one-year-old baby." "Well...yes..." I said with a sidelong glance at my husband, angling for, certain of, his approval. "But what does she *do*?" The woman quite rightly turned her back on me. But my husband beamed. And I, knowing full well the extent of my unforgivable rudeness, shamelessly basked in the cherished instant of his approval. I knew I had behaved abominably. At that moment, I did not care.

∞

It is the tiny acts of betrayal — of friends, of family, of self — that are the true legacy of abuse. Not the dramatic emergency room confrontations, but the daily diminishments, each as tiny and insignificant as a raindrop, that — drop by drop — erode a woman's soul.

This is why abuse always has an aftermath. A woman who has survived becomes as vigilant as a combat infantryman, determined to protect herself from further danger. She may not realize that she is doing so. Dawn believed that she had overcome her past, as though the will to do so meant that it no longer existed. Preserved as if in amber, it remained, a hard little lump, tucked in a dark corner of a locked cupboard in a high attic in a lonely house in a remote village. She broke free of her abusive husband after only three years. It took sixteen years before she could trust sufficiently to remarry. Even then, there was still, and may be yet, a part of her mind that remained steadfastly on patrol, remembering the injuries, ready to repel any possibility of new hurts.

Replaying any traumatic event — a rape, a car wreck, a mugging, a war — is both common and healing. The mind chews diligently on the indigestible lump of the trauma, sometimes for months, sometimes for years. After I left, I would conduct lengthy imaginary conversations with Melvin. Calm, rational conversations that magically thinned his anger.

I would set up the chess pieces of a past battle, recollecting in vivid detail what I had done (as though I had done something to merit his abuse), how he had responded (as though his responses were somehow justified), and how I had reacted (as though my reaction could have made a difference). Then I would replay the interaction, giving myself new lines, new strategies, watching as I magically transformed his impatience to amusement, his anger to approval. These conversations persisted for nearly twenty years. They persisted until I believed that I was, indeed I had been for some time, safe.

Section IV
Letting Go. Going On.

There is a myth that battered women either return to their abuser or find another to replace him. This sometimes happens, of course. But most women successfully escape and go forward with their lives. Many achieve stunning professional and personal triumphs.

We believe we've made progress by calling these women "survivors" instead of "victims." But in doing so, we lose sight of the fact that these were once simply people. Little girls. Teenagers. Women. The women whose stories appear in this section have all spent time and energy struggling to understand, to draw meaning from the abuse. Ultimately, they have all found ways to reconstruct their lives.

10
Jesusa Fox

I Am Picturing the Future

Because he lied in the court, I lost the custody battle.
And I said to the judge, this is a beating, another
beating, not from my husband, but from the system.

"You know, the first time when I leave home I think to myself, 'I am crazy.' I feel like, 'No, I have to go to the mental hospital, not the shelter.' Because he always tell me I am crazy." Jesusa leans toward me, her eyes searching mine, checking to see if I understand. "Yes, they do that, don't they," I reply. She nods vigorously, satisfied. We smile at each other across the table that occupies a corner of my tiny room in this bed and breakfast inn on the outskirts of Charleston, South Carolina. I am in Charleston to teach a workshop for medical students. The faculty member who arranged my visit also volunteers at the local battered women's shelter. She told the director of the shelter about my book. The director talked to Jesusa, and now Jesusa is talking to me.

These days, Jesusa is talking to many people about domestic abuse. After twelve years of silence and secrecy, she believes it is time for her to speak up. On this Sunday morning she has just given a talk at her Catholic church. Then she took two busses to get to my inn. Jesusa has a driver's license, but she has no car. The car was only one of many possessions she had to abandon a year ago when she escaped from Hank. She left without her furniture, her clothes, her makeup, and her naturalization papers. She also left without her four-year-old and six-year-old sons. Jesusa's husband, an ex-Marine, is an American citizen. Jesusa is a citizen as well, but she was born in the Philippines. Hank threatened to have her deported if she took the boys to the shelter and she, unfamiliar with naturalization laws, believed he had the power to do so.

This was not the first time Jesusa had attempted to escape from Hank. "I leave four times, I stay in the shelter four times, but the first three times I feel guilty and I go home. I always think he will change, he will choose to be good to me. But he don't change. The third time I went home he is using God towards me. He says the demon is in you…we're gonna go to the priest to take out the demon. Just barely did I believe him that I have the demon inside, but then I realize, no! He is the demon!"

The fourth time Jesusa left she did not feel guilty; she felt angry. She believes it was her anger that gave her the strength to leave, even though leaving her home also meant leaving her children. Jesusa was optimistic that one of Charleston's legal-aid attorneys could defend her from Hank's threat of deportation. She had learned, during a prior stay at the shelter, that a battered woman could receive free legal assistance. She imagined that after a few weeks at the shelter, a few weeks of peace where her body and spirit could heal, she and her sons would move to an apartment and live safely apart from Hank. But the day Jesusa went to the shelter, Hank filed for sole custody. He claimed that Jesusa was an unfit mother. He cited, among a litany of lies, one inarguable truth: she had abandoned the children.

Jesusa draws a shaky breath. This is a part of her life that will never be made whole. She admits that when she was living at home she sometimes found it difficult to take care of the boys. "He was degrading me all the time, on and on shouting. He will not work, he's just around me day and night. I'm happy when he's going out, I'm happy because I can spend time with the children. But when he's around he's just constantly screaming. Or he didn't like what I said, and then he's slapping me, or choking me, or even putting a plastic bag on my face."

Slight of build, Jesusa was easy for Hank to overpower. He twisted her arm behind her back so viciously, and so frequently, that her ligaments sustained permanent injury. She extends her arm to show me the damage: with her elbow locked at an awkward angle, she cannot lift her hand above her head. The hovering menace of Hank's mistreatment eventually affected Jesusa's abilities as a mother. When the boys misbehaved, she found herself screaming at them until they ran to their room in tears. Horrified at herself, she would fly after them: "Sorry, sorry, Mommy didn't mean it, Mommy has lots going on in her mind." The older boy would hug her. "He says, 'I love you, Mommy.' And that breaks my heart, because instead of me comforting him, he became the comfort to me."

At the custody hearing, Jesusa's lawyer attempted to fight Hank's claims with a counter-accusation of domestic violence. However, since Jesusa had never filed a police report, there was no evidence that such violence had ever taken place. Jesusa tried to explain: had she called the police, she knew that Hank would have beaten her even more severely. Hank also delighted in taunting her: no cop, he insisted, would ever side with her against a former Marine. Caught between her fear of Hank and her fear of a police officer's disbelief, Jesusa felt she had no choice but to tolerate the abuse in silence. Although Jesusa's lawyer did his best to present his client's case, the judge was not convinced. Jesusa will never forget the way Hank's lawyer framed it. "Your Honor, the abuse is just a figment of her imagination." Jesusa spits her words bitterly. "Because he lied in the court, I lost the custody battle. And I said to the judge, this is a beating, another beating, not from my husband, but from the system."

I ask Jesusa how she found the strength to keep going after this stunning defeat. A devout Catholic, she firmly believes that Hank may have won in Charleston family court, but that he will not win in the court of God. "I always thank God for everything that has happened to me. He is the one who give me courage to get out. Even though it meant leaving my children now, it will not be for always. I think the hardest decision I make in my life was to leave my children to the person who beat me up." Hank never used violence against the boys, but they often witnessed his violence against their mother. Until recently, Jesusa assumed that she was the only victim of Hank's abuse, but at the shelter her counselor gave her a book about the children of battered women. Now she worries about what she sees when she looks into her sons' faces. During her weekly court-ordered visits, she does what she can to counter the unspoken lessons they have learned at home. "I don't want them to think this is a normal life. I want them to know that this is not good…this is wrong…hitting is crime. And I tell them you're going to go to jail if you hit. I look at them and say, 'Did you understand that?'" I think, though I do not say, that while Jesusa's sons may understand her words, they also know what they saw. Their father hit…and their father is not in jail.

Jesusa was raised with the message she now tries to teach her sons. Her mother died when Jesusa was three; when her father died nine years later, her aunt and uncle took her in. She felt lucky to be surrounded by good people; in her neighborhood, she saw many other families that were not so lucky. "I think to myself: I don't want to be a bad one...I always strive to be respected, to obey the rules." She met Hank when she was in her late teens. A Marine Lance Corporal, he was stationed at a military base a few miles from her town. She trusted him immediately because he exhibited the same gentleness she had seen in her father and her uncle.

Hank and Jesusa were married in the Philippines and remained there for nearly a year. Jesusa remembers this as a happy time. Then, when Hank's tour of duty was up, they moved back to the States. In Charleston, Jesusa was thousands of miles from the people who would have protected her. And that was when the beatings started. "I told my husband he was like my father. But the first time he started putting his hand on my neck, he's not like my father. My father told us, 'Don't hit!' I say to Hank then, you're not like my father."

Jesusa lost the custody battle, but she has not given up hope. Her lawyer is continuing to fight on her behalf. She is also working to muster community support. She visits churches and community gatherings, telling her story to anyone who will listen. Some offer to help; she refuses to be discouraged by the others. She has a touching faith that, eventually, everything will work out for the best. Already, she has reclaimed much of the self she lost during her marriage. She recalls the person she was a year ago, when she entered the shelter for the fourth and last time: "You are like a robot. You don't have self-esteem, you're numb, you don't have feeling. You have a shattered image." Jesusa has spent the past twelve months slowly reassembling the fragments of that image. She has moved from the shelter to a transition apartment owned by the Salvation Army, where she lives rent-free in exchange for kitchen duties. She still attends support group meetings, teaching as well as learning. Recently the women in her group were asked to draw pictures of their past, their present, and their future. Jesusa sketches these for me in the air; I see them as clearly as if they were on the table beside my tape recorder.

Jesusa's first drawing showed her past: a steep rocky mountain enveloped by a thick cloud. The mountain, she tells me, represents how she felt during her marriage: struggling to please, struggling to accommodate, while the murky cloud obscured the rocks that, inevitably, sent her tumbling to the bottom of the mountain. Again and again she would attempt the climb; again and again she would trip and fall.

Her second drawing — her present — contained two symbols. First she drew a bird, the image of freedom. In the space beside the bird she sketched a dog, which she associates with peace of mind. These, she says, are where she is standing right now. Now that she is free, and her mind is at peace, she feels ready to move toward the future.

Jesusa's drawing of the future is stuffed so full that the page can barely contain the images of her dreams. Noah's dove of peace. Herself, drawn large, a whole person. A heart, her own full heart, radiates lines that reach out toward the two small figures of her sons. A yellow sun with a smiling face represents her bright future. An arrow points from a large green dollar sign to the house she plans to buy some day, where she and her children can live together. A flower garden surrounds a solid rock, which portrays the stability of her job. A chimney on one side of the house makes it a place of warmth and comfort; a place where she, her children, and perhaps even other abused women can feel safe. There are mountains in the distance, where she and her children will travel some day. And, arched over the whole, a rainbow: her faith that God will help her make this future real.

As the interview draws to an end, I ask Jesusa a final question. I have, of course, met men named Jesus, but I have never met a woman named Jesusa. Is this a common name in the Philippines? It is because of her birthday, she explains. She was born on Christmas Day. "That's my birthday, too!" I exclaim. We dig in our handbags for our driver's licenses, placing them side by side on the table. My image and hers stare up at me from the plastic rectangles: December 25, 1947; December 25, 1956. My junior by nine years. My sister. We hug, and promise to send each other birthday cards next year. Several weeks later, an envelope arrives from Charleston. It contains a religious card, a brief note, and a gift. Jesusa has designed — and convinced a local jeweler to create — yet another symbol. A thin ring, a spiral of silver whose ends do not meet. "It is a broken circle," she writes, "to remind women that we have to break the cycle." I wear Jesusa's ring whenever I write or speak about domestic abuse. I am wearing it today.

❧ Reflection ❧

Freedom does not always announce itself with parades and fireworks. For Jesusa, one of the best parts of leaving has been the freedom to do needlepoint. Hank had forbidden her to "waste time" on this innocuous hobby. The sight of her, bent contentedly over a brightly-patterned canvas when she should have been tending to his needs, would send him into a rage. She learned to do her stitching in secret. When she heard him at the front door, she hurriedly rolled the canvas and tucked it safely under the bed. Such a tiny symbol. So essential. Imagine for a moment what it would be like to live under such constant surveillance.

For me, leaving meant the freedom to stand naked, combing my hair in front of a full-length mirror, knowing that Melvin wouldn't suddenly appear behind me, shaking his head in despair at the size of my hips, putting a hand at each side of my waist and pulling viciously backward to show me how I ought to look, how thin I ought to be.

You'd think, wouldn't you, that it would have been something much more dramatic. Freedom from slaps, from kicks, from belligerent sex. Instead, it was the sheer, utter, exhilarating relief of being free to simply be…without being constantly on my guard.

The summer after I left Melvin, he began a messy little affair with my friend Sheila. Messy because, although she and her husband were in the midst of a bumpy patch, they were still married. I learned of the affair quite by accident the day Sheila came to my apartment for lunch. She told me that she had spent the morning with Melvin. At the moment, it didn't occur to me that she had spent the previous night there as well. When I served lunch — cream of tomato soup, crackers, and a platter of fresh vegetables — Sheila surveyed the table glumly. Then, with a tense frown, she reached for a celery stick. As I sipped my soup and nibbled crackers, she paced herself, reaching every five minutes for a single carrot, a thin cucumber slice, or a pale green stalk of celery. By the time our lunch was over, she had consumed no more than fifty calories worth of food. She shuddered visibly at the little plate of gingersnap cookies I placed beside the teapot, and refused my offer of milk or sugar.

Sheila was neither plump nor model-thin. At five feet three inches, she had, for the ten years I had known her, weighed a pleasant 120 pounds. Like every woman alive, she wished that five pounds would magically disappear overnight. Still, she fit easily into a size ten dress and had never wasted much energy dreaming about an unattainable size six. Her round Slavic face could have graced a magazine ad for buttermilk. Now, though, I discerned faint hollows in cheeks that were no longer rosy.

And then, with a sudden flash of insight, I knew. I knew they were sleeping together. And I knew that Melvin had begun to chip away at Sheila's vision of herself. I could practically hear his words. First, he would have praised Sheila's voluptuous curves. Then, ever so gently, ever so kindly, he would have asked if perhaps she worried about her weight. Not that she was fat — but hadn't she ever wished she could wear skintight jeans and a snug tank top? He sure would like to see her in a sexy outfit like that. Not that she wasn't already sexy — but she could look so much better. Just fifteen pounds would make such a difference. And it wouldn't even be that hard to do!

All she had to do was pay just a tiny bit more attention to what she ate.

All she had to do was give up her freedom to eat what she pleased.

On average, battered women return to their batterers five times before they escape for good. Jesusa made it in four. Each time she left the shelter and moved back to their house, she hoped that Hank had changed. And each time, her hopes were dashed. Jesusa must have felt like a failure, blaming herself for believing Hank's promises, blaming herself for repeating the pattern that had characterized their marriage. However — and this is the key to understanding the process by which a battered woman extricates herself — through the act of leaving, Jesusa learned that she *could* leave.

She learned, for example, that the shelter was a safe place to hide from Hank. She learned that counselors would take the time to listen, that social workers would help her find affordable housing, that doctors and lawyers would offer their services without charge. She learned that Hank's threat to deport her was without substance. She learned that she had legal rights; that she could fight Hank for custody of her sons. She learned that her behavior was not causing Hank's beatings. She learned that his attacks were not motivated by anger, but by a need to gain power and control. She learned that she was not alone; that other women were tangled in similar webs of physical and psychological abuse.

All this knowledge gave her a new perspective on her marriage. Yes, Hank managed to lure her back three times. But it was an increasingly confident woman who returned to him. Each time, she was further from the center of the web, until she finally freed herself.

11
Lillia Lopez

I Am Making a Difference

*I re-brainwashed myself. The counselors at the shelter
told me I had been brainwashed into believing that I was
no good. I thought: Okay, I'm gonna get a new hairdo,
I'm gonna get new clothes. I started to jog every night for
an hour, and during my jogging, I fed myself positive
things like I'm intelligent, I'm beautiful, I am loving, I
am loved, I am wonderful, I am happy and successful.*

The woman on the stage is wearing a dramatic dress, jet
black with one vivid red strip that begins at her right shoulder
and runs diagonally to her left knee. Her glossy red lipstick is
the exact shade of her high-heeled shoes. She is poised and
impeccably professional. Then she begins to tell her story.
Suddenly she is sobbing, her mascara making smudgy little
rivers down her cheeks. It is, I learn subsequently, not at all
unusual for her to fall apart midsentence. Though her five-
year abusive marriage ended thirteen years ago, she cannot
revisit the facts without reliving the emotions. She reaches for
Kleenex after Kleenex as she walks the audience through the
beatings, the emergency room visits, the threats with a loaded
pistol. Telling her story is not an exercise in wallowing self-
pity…it is what she does for a living. She is a victim advocate,
a member of the Tennessee Domestic Violence Coalition. She

works with victims of rape, domestic abuse, armed robbery, and other assault crimes. She is good at her job, because she understands what it is to be a victim.

Her name is Guadalupe Lilliana Theresa Lopez. Everyone but her grandmother calls her Lillia. The daughter of migrant farm workers, Lillia's goal was to make something of herself. "My parents were from Mexico, but I was born in North Dakota. See, my parents were poor. At that time in their lives, they traveled around to different places doing different kinds of fieldwork. And it just so happened that my mother was real pregnant when the potato crop was in, so I was born there. Then they left, so even though it's on my birth certificate and all, I've never even seen North Dakota!"

When Lillia was six, her father got a job with the railroad, settled his family in Corpus Christi, Texas, and became a United States citizen. Citizenship allowed him to sponsor the many members of the Lopez family eagerly waiting to emigrate from Mexico. As a result, Lillia grew up surrounded by grandparents, aunts, uncles, and cousins. She never felt a sense of deprivation; her memories of her childhood are benignly happy. There was the playground where she and her three sisters jumped rope and navigated the monkey bars. The fresh fish her brothers caught in the Gulf of Mexico and brought home for the family's dinner. The schoolteachers who nurtured their many Spanish-speaking students, who saw to it that Lillia was fully bilingual by the time she was eight. Only a faint lilting blurriness at the end of her sentences alerts a careful listener that English was not Lillia's first language. "One time after I had grown up my mother was telling me how poor we were. And I'm going, 'Mother, I can't believe that!' Because I felt like we had such a fun childhood. For me it was just so much fun, but I never, ever realized we were so poor."

School was an obligation, like Sunday Mass and Wednesday afternoon Catechism classes, to be endured with as much good grace as possible. What Lillia liked best about school were the extracurricular activities. She joined the Brownies in first grade, and graduated from high school a dedicated Girl Scout. She helped organize Corpus Christie High School's football fund-raising drive, selling more candy each year than any other student. A junior high school Civics teacher inspired her interest in politics. "Politics was always one of my greatest loves. I didn't run for anything, but I always volunteered for one campaign or another, even as a high school student. I remember, you know, telling my parents who they should vote for. I couldn't hardly wait to get to vote myself."

After high school, Lillia went to work for J.C. Penney, the largest and most popular department store in Corpus Christi. An attractive girl with a ready smile and a bubbling enthusiasm, she soon became known for her record sales at the perfume counter. Within a year, she was managing the entire cosmetics department. Whenever she gets a job, Lillia reflects, she instinctively knows how to get herself promoted in record time. "But when I was younger, I changed jobs often. I look back and I think, why? I could have been running the whole store by now. I guess I got bored fast."

A few months later, Lillia married. She and Jimmy had known each other for six years, though they had only dated for two; when they met, she was a pudgy twelve-year-old with a big crush on eighteen-year-old Jimmy, who in turn had a crush on one of Lillia's older sisters. "Then when I was sixteen and he was twenty-one, he all of a sudden took a look at me said, 'Wow, did you grow up cute!'" When Lillia turned seventeen, Jimmy proposed. "I married him just after high school. But we didn't really know each other that well, because for the two years we were dating, he was in the Army. We wrote all these lovey-dovey letters, but we only saw each other when he was home on leave. It was real romantic and all, but knowing what I know now, I can see I was way too young and spoiled to get married."

Jimmy, Lillia assures me, was a good husband and father. The problem was not Jimmy himself, but Lillia's vision of what Jimmy ought to be. "He had no ambition. He was content with his job, so if he'd get a thirty-cents-an-hour raise, he'd be, like, look at that! But every time I had a job, I would be promoted immediately. He didn't like that, because it meant that I spent more time away from home." After three years, Lillia decided she was tired of waiting for Jimmy to make something of himself. The divorce was, she concedes, largely her fault. She was immature. She had had her heart set on this man since she was twelve years old; once she had him, she no longer wanted him. "I was a very selfish, self-centered, spoiled brat," she says with a wry smile. "I probably hurt him, but I'm sorry to say that at the time, his feelings never even crossed my mind."

Lillia was tired of the department store; she needed a new challenge. A family friend had just been made the night manager of a large hotel in Miami and offered her a job working the night shift at the front desk. She packed up her clothes and her two-year-old son, Buddy, and off they went. Once again, she moved quickly up the management ladder. Soon she was working days; within a year, she was the front desk manager. She and Buddy stayed in Miami for three years. Then it was on to Jacksonville, where she worked her way up from nightclub hostess to nightclub manager. Two years later, she moved to Atlanta, where she ran a large art gallery. "I was young and I could just, you know, I had no fear of anything."

She was twenty-nine years old and had been cheerfully single for eight years. One day a man came into the art gallery. His name was Tony Laudato. "The Perpetrator," she calls him, startling me with the bald, uncompromising, police-blotter expression. "My ex-husband, the perpetrator, was a salesman. He went all around the South doing trade shows." Tony was in Atlanta for the week, staffing a booth at the convention center around the corner from Lillia's art gallery. He began dropping in several times a day: before the show opened, during his coffee breaks, during lunch, and in the late afternoon. "Through the whole show, he kept asking me to go out with him, and I kept sayin' no… no… no… no… no… NO! I had just broken up from a relationship of three years, and I had no desire to go out with this man. Finally on the last day of the show he asked me out again, and I thought, okay, well, he's gonna go, he's leaving tomorrow, so I went out with him."

Over dinner Tony talked to her about his work, his recent divorce (he neglected to mention two previous failed marriages), his son (though he managed to forget that he also had four children by his first two wives), and his religion. "He was Church of Christ, which I really didn't know anything about, being raised Catholic. Anyway, he was quite charming, and I thought that would be the end of it, that I'd never see him again." Tony went back to Memphis and started calling Lillia once, twice, three times a day. He was as persistent as he had been when he invited her to dinner in Atlanta…only this time, he had raised the stakes. He wanted her to marry him. "I kept saying: 'No, Tony! I don't even know you!' I was happy with my life in Atlanta. I was content, I was very self-confident, I thought I was really something special. But he kept asking me to marry him and marry him, calling me all day long. I couldn't even put the phone down at my apartment. As soon as I'd put the phone down it would ring again and, you know, it was him."

Thirteen days of Tony's unremitting phone siege finally wore Lillia down. She still isn't sure quite how it happened, but she heard herself agreeing to marry him. "And the next thing I know, I'm in the car with my sister, being driven to the airport, on my way to Memphis to get married. And I can remember feeling like I was in some kind of a fog and thinking: Oh gosh, I'm so crazy…why am I doing this?"

I picture Lillia transplanted to Memphis, away from her closely-knit family, married to a traveling salesman who is barely home long enough to change his socks, and who, in any case, she barely knows. I picture her wearing a hat and gloves every Sunday, Buddy in a crisp white shirt, the two of them sitting sedately in the Church of Christ chapel beside Tony's mother and sister. The unfamiliar liturgy must have seemed as alien to mother and son as her new husband, his new father. I picture her boredom: Lillia had worked since she was seventeen; now she was married to a man who wanted her to stay safely at home. Why, he challenged, did she want a job? He made plenty of money. Enough to buy her whatever she needed. All she had to do was ask — and he'd dole out twenty-dollar bills, one at a time, until the stack reached what was, in his eyes, a sufficient amount.

Shortly after Lillia moved to Memphis, her mother died. The two had been extremely close, talking on the phone three or four times a week. "After her death, if I cried or if I was somber, he'd say, 'What's wrong with you?' I'd say, 'I just miss my mother,' and he'd say, 'Well, you know, you've done enough grieving and it's time for you to go on with your life.' Now in my work as a victim advocate, I hear this from other victims. Not being allowed to grieve…it's not that unusual." Tony, like all abusive men, had to know that he had Lillia's full attention at all times. He could not tolerate the possibility that she cared for, thought about, anyone other than him.

Tony's psychological abuse started a few months after their wedding. Within a year, he had taken to slapping her, "…and then it started escalating. I had bruises on my arms from where he'd hold on and shake me. Once I had a black eye, and I was so embarrassed I wouldn't leave the house for two weeks. I told his mother and sister that I had the flu." She heard rumors that Tony was seeing a woman in Nashville. Then she heard rumors of a second woman in Little Rock. It didn't take Lillia long to realize Tony rarely took a business trip alone. She learned not to call him at his hotel room; her pride would not allow her to run the risk of hearing another woman's voice answer the telephone.

They had been married three years when Lillia became pregnant. Tony's beatings became increasingly frequent and violent. He would pull her around the house by her hair. He would drag her off the sofa when he caught her napping in the middle of the day. "It was the only kind of touching I got from him because he didn't even want to have sex with me. He told me I was ugly. He called me a pig. I wasn't even fat. While I was at my heaviest with Stephanie, I weighed 134 pounds. I mean, I weigh more than that now!"

After Stephanie was born, Tony's abuse took a new and frightening turn. He began to threaten her with a loaded pistol. He was always calm during one of these episodes. Carefully, with almost ritualistic precision, he would spread newspaper on the dining room table. Then he would methodically take his pistol apart, setting each blue-gray piece of metal down on the newspaper. With an oily rag, he would polish each until it gleamed. Then he would reassemble the weapon, put one bullet in the chamber, and point the barrel at Lillia's head. Sometimes he would pull the trigger, laughing at the harmless click as the hammer encountered an empty chamber. "Each time, I was sure I was going to die. After a while, I wished I would. I just wanted him to kill me and get it over with."

A newspaper article ultimately shook Lillia out of her lethargy. The headline read "Hunting Season Bags Unintended Victims." The article described the increase in cases of domestic violence during hunting season. It featured an interview with the director of Safe House, a battered women's shelter in downtown Memphis. "I never knew that one existed before that, ever anywhere. I never knew anyone but myself, you know, that this had happened to." The article ended with the shelter's telephone number. Lillia took her nail scissors and cut a careful square, neatly extracting the telephone number. She hid the tiny scrap in the linen closet between the shelf paper and the shelf.

Lillia did not take immediate action. But just knowing the fragment of paper was in her linen closet seemed to energize her. Now and then, when Tony was away, she'd open the closet and read the phone number to herself. That was all. But it was enough. In April, seven months after she had read the article, she asked Tony for a divorce. "I just finally thought, this is it. I've had it. I just don't want to go through this anymore."

Tony didn't go into a rage. Instead, he conducted his pistol-cleaning ceremony, with, if possible, even more care and precision than usual. He put the customary bullet in the chamber. Then, to Lillia's horror, he went over to the crib, scooped up one-year-old Stephanie, and pointed the gun at her head. "Now I want you to tell me again," he said with icy calm, "that you want a divorce." Lillia fell at his feet and begged. She would do anything he wanted, she said. Anything. She would stay with him forever. She would never divorce him. She babbled whatever words she had to say, until he slowly lowered the pistol. "Any emotions that I had for him — because during this time I still did have emotions for him — any good emotions that I had for him were severed, right there. The minute I saw him holding a gun to that little girl's head, that was it. When he did that, it was…I'm not gonna *ask* him for a divorce. I'm gonna *get* one."

Lillia took the scrap of paper from its hiding place and called the battered women's shelter. The next day, she and the two children moved in. She cannot say enough good things about Safe House. The weeks she spent there changed her life. "They treated me so well, they just were great. In my work now, I talk to other victims and they say, 'Lillia, you mean you went to the shelter? That place is horrible. It's a horrible place to stay and live.' Well, sure, it was old and dingy. But it was my castle. I even remember the room that I had. It was in the front, on the second floor. I remember the sunlight coming through the window, and I just thought…this is like a fortress to me because nothing can penetrate it."

Tony knew, or at least suspected, that she and the children had fled to Safe House. He began calling there at all hours of the day and night, asking, pleading, begging to talk to his wife. When the well-trained telephone receptionist told him to put a bug in his ear, he began to make threats. "I'm coming down there, and I'm gonna get her out," he warned. Lillia was terrified. She sat in the shelter director's office, shaking. "You don't know this guy. If he says he's gonna get me, then he's gonna get me. He's dangerous!" The director just smiled. "She told me, 'Let him try. *Nobody* gets past that front door.' And that's what made me realize, you know, that it was a fortress, that it was a safe place. It was the safest place for Buddy and Stephanie and me to be."

The shelter kept her body safe, but once she was free of Tony's daily threats and beatings, she started to appreciate how much damage had been done to her mind. A social worker at the shelter helped her understand the extent to which Tony had whittled away at her confidence. "I was so brainwashed that I believed the whole world was bad. I was in a state of mind where I thought I was never gonna be free. I had been brainwashed so much that it was almost like I was in a tunnel and I was watching a movie through this tunnel." What, I ask Lillia, was the movie about? "It was a movie of me. I was viewing myself from the outside. I was going through the motions, only it wasn't me. It was me there in the movie going through the motions, and I was watching myself do it."

The same social worker asked Lillia if she believed all men were abusers like Tony. Yes, Lillia responded, I truly believe they are. No, the social worker replied, they aren't. There are any number of good men in the world, men who do not batter, men who do not need to control a relationship. In fact, the counselor continued, she had found one of them. "She told me that she had been in an abusive relationship before she was married to this husband, that now she had a wonderful marriage with her new husband, and that my life could change just like hers did. And at that moment, it was like my whole chest opened up and I just thought: Oh, my gosh, I can have a normal life! She gave me hope that my life could be different. She told me, I made it, and you can make it. She gave me hope."

All battered women's shelters have waiting lists and, consequently, time limits. A woman and her children cannot remain there forever. There are too many other women and children who need a safe place to hide from a violent man. The Memphis shelter has a maximum stay of four weeks. After that, though a woman is free to return for counseling and advice, she must find housing elsewhere. Lillia left after three weeks. She saved the remaining seven days the way I used to save my Halloween candy. If she needed them later, if she and the children found themselves in serious trouble, the extra seven days in the fortress would be her secret weapon against Tony.

As it happened, she never returned to the shelter, never used her secret store of days. Tony stalked her, appearing unannounced in the restaurant where she waited tables, lingering in the parking lot of the grocery store where she did her marketing, but she never felt in real danger. Now that she is working with other battered women, she acknowledges how fortunate she was. At the time, she didn't know the statistics. She thought her protective order and her deadbolt lock would keep her safe. "Ignorance is bliss, I guess. I'm almost glad I didn't know how many women like me get killed after they leave."

One of the counselors at the shelter had helped Lillia find the job in the restaurant. She had to work a double shift to earn enough money for rent and food. She had no car. An hour each way on the bus added to a full work day meant she was away from her baby daughter ten to twelve hours a day. Childcare was a serious concern. Lillia doesn't know how she would have managed without her son. "Buddy was fifteen. He would take Stephanie to daycare and then go to school. Then he would come from school, pick her up at daycare, and bring her home. He would give her a bath and feed her and put her to sleep. He was just wonderful. He was just the best little guy that I had."

Stephanie has no memories of that time. No memories of her father's violence, of the room at the shelter, of the months when her brother took over so her mother could work. But Buddy, now in his late twenties, remembers his stepfather all too well. "We talk about it now and he says, 'Yeah, Mom, I remember laying in my bed cryin' because I would hear him beating up on you.' There were several times where he tried to interfere, and he would get beat up in the process. So I would just tell Buddy...I would beg him not to help me because I was afraid that he would get hurt."

Lillia was thirty-five when she escaped. Five years with Tony had drained her self-worth to the point where no one would have recognized the woman who once confidently mastered job after job. She barely recognized that woman herself. What steps did she take, I ask, to reconstruct herself? Lillia smiles at the memory. "You know what I did? I re-brainwashed myself! Because the counselors at the shelter told me I had been brainwashed into believing that I was no good. I thought: Okay, I'm gonna get a new hairdo, I'm gonna get new clothes, he took all the antique furniture, so I'm gonna like contemporary, I'm gonna go totally the opposite. I started to jog every night for an hour, and during my jogging, I fed myself positive things like I'm intelligent, I'm beautiful, I am loving, I am loved, I am wonderful, I am happy and successful. And you know what? I became all those things again."

Lillia believes that religion helped her as she worked to rebuild her life. After her divorce, she returned to Catholicism. The Church of Christ services she had attended for five years out of deference to Tony's family were simply one more piece of her history that she was eager to leave behind. She took comfort in the familiar rituals of Sunday Mass, associated as they were with her pleasant memories of childhood. "Ever since I was a child, I knew that God was a driving person in my life. You hear people saying, 'God help me; why have You made me go through this?' I don't believe in that. If anything, maybe God guided me in this direction so that I can do what I'm doing now. Maybe He wanted me to experience this so that I can help the people I am helping now."

Lillia gets calls from battered women every day. They are upset. They are angry. They are often hysterical. "I know," she tells them. "I believe you." The voice on the other end of the phone will pause. "You mean," the caller will falter, "you don't think I'm crazy?" "No," replies Lillia, "I don't think you're crazy. I believe you. I know just what you're going through. I've been there."

❧ Reflection ❧

You are walking through a beautiful forest. Birds are singing. The sun is shining. Suddenly, you fall into a deep pit that you never even realized was in front of you. "How did I get here?" you wonder. "Everything was so lovely." You are disoriented from the fall, slightly injured, and very much alone. You call for help, but nobody answers. You try to crawl out, but the man at the surface pushes you back down. Each time this happens, you feel a little more disoriented.

It is, of course, possible to climb out of the pit. But not without resources. A job. A good friend who listens without judging. A doctor who recognizes the signs and symptoms of abuse, and who does not turn away. A policeman who tells you, then proves to you, that the law is on your side. Lillia speaks glowingly of the police officers that kept an eye on her after she had filed a protective order. "All I had to do was call," she remembers, "and they would come by in their cruiser."

I am a volunteer with the Utah State Attorney General's "Safe at Home" program. This is a one-hour presentation that brings a videotape, a facilitator, and one or more domestic violence professionals to the workplace, carrying the message of domestic violence prevention to factories, offices, hospitals, and schools. I serve as facilitator, which means it is my job to make sure that the videotape is rewound, the pamphlets are distributed, and all audience questions are answered. Donkey work. I am glad to do it — glad to leave the speeches to the experts. Often the expert is one of the well-trained sheriffs from the Salt Lake County Domestic Violence Unit.

Police have, in the past, received a lot of bad press for failing to properly intervene in domestic violence assaults. "Punch and Judy Shows," police officers called these, often doing little more than giving both parties a "good talking to" and sending the batterer for a walk around the block to "cool down." Nowadays, in most states, most of the time, the law enforcement response has improved dramatically. At a recent Safe at Home session, my co-presenter was a police lieutenant. The audience was left in no doubt of his position on domestic violence. Shaking a warning finger, he concluded with these words: "The law says, *you* beat up your wife, *I* get to haul your ugly butt to jail."

A woman may remain with a batterer for years, enduring unspeakable assaults on her body and mind. She will leave when she gives up the dream. When she says to herself, "I don't want it any more. I'm through. He's a mean, nasty, evil person. I'm not going to be abused any more."

What makes a woman give up the dream? For some, like Lillia, it is an event as dramatic and terrifying as seeing a loaded gun pointing at her child's head. For others, it can be a surprisingly small gesture. An Israeli woman sent me an e-mail letter describing her wake-up call, which came after thirty years of marriage. At the family's Passover seder, a religious event which, ironically, celebrates freedom from bondage, she and her husband sat at the large dining room table surrounded by family and friends. The focus of a seder is the retelling, in prayer and song, of the story of Moses and the exodus from Egypt. Because the holiday is celebrated in the home rather than the synagogue, every seder is different. Each family has its own traditions: a well-loved story, a special prayer, a favorite song. When this woman expressed the wish to sing a particular song, her husband turned and said, "Behave!" Her letter continued, "I thought to myself, one only says 'Behave' to three-year-olds and dogs. I am neither."

Passover is celebrated in the spring. She left that summer.

12
Maryellen Kasimian

I Am Stronger Than Ever

*When I woke up in the hospital, I knew that I didn't
deserve what he had been doing to me for all those
years. It wasn't right, it wasn't my fault, and there was
no way I'd ever want to be around him again.*

Maryellen strides briskly into the conference room. One
hand clasps a tuna sandwich. The other reaches out to shake
mine. She is slightly out of breath, having rushed over to meet
with me on her lunch break. She laughs as she tells me not to
worry: she can talk quite well with her mouth full.

The daughter of a pharmacist, Maryellen Kasimian had
dreamed of being a physician for as long as she could remember. When she was four years old, she pestered her father until
he finally parted with a tongue depressor, two ace bandages,
and an old pair of tweezers. These were Maryellen's surgical
tools. She would roam the neighborhood in search of patients,
taking temperatures, dislodging splinters, and wrapping bandages around the knee or elbow of anyone she could convince
to hold still. At home, however, Maryellen learned not to talk
about her ambition. Her parents made it very clear that little
girls didn't grow up to be doctors. They grow up to be wives
and mothers.

Ashmir Kasimian's family had immigrated to Tulsa from Armenia when he was in junior high school. In 1950 he met Sheila Hamilton at a sorority party. They married six months later, the weekend of Ashmir's graduation. Their daughter, Janine, was born that year. Maryellen was born fifteen months later, Patricia was born the following year, and Andrew was born two years later.

Ashmir treated his wife and children with absentminded kindness. And if Sheila got out of control now and then, there were always tranquilizers to help her manage her day. As a pharmacist, Ashmir could obtain these easily enough. The atmosphere in the Kasimian house was generally calm, if somewhat remote. But when Maryellen was five, Sheila snapped. She grabbed the bottle of tranquilizers and announced, "My life is ruined. I hate you goddamned kids. I'll take all these pills, and then I'll die, and then your father will be sorry." The children stood frozen as their mother dashed into the bathroom and swallowed about thirty of the little yellow tablets. Ashmir bundled his wife into the front seat of his car and sped to the hospital where Sheila's stomach was pumped. When their father arrived home that night, he gathered the four children around him and solemnly announced that "Mama needs a rest." The children were sent to live with their grandparents for the month that Sheila spent in the psychiatric ward.

Sheila attempted suicide about once a year. The pattern was always the same: a long period of relative tranquillity followed by a violent emotional outburst and several weeks in an institution. She probably suffered from a severe form of seasonal depression. At the time, though, Maryellen was convinced that she, and she alone, was responsible for her mother's unhappiness. She examined her actions in excruciating detail. If she could just discover the secret of how to be a perfect little girl, she reasoned, her mother wouldn't take the pills that sent her away.

As Sheila's depression steadily worsened, Maryellen found a small quiet place within herself and shrank to fit inside it. By the time she turned fourteen, the bossy neighborhood doctor had become a painfully shy bookworm who found home and school equally unbearable. Home held Sheila, with her constant need to be placated and her mysteriously unpredictable rages. School, once the safe haven of a girls-only Christian school, was now a public high school with something even more frightening than her mother. Boys. "I couldn't look people in the eye," Maryellen remembers. "That was the first time I was around boys, and I was so shy I thought I'd die."

Maryellen never overcame that shyness. Three years of high school passed with few friends, fewer parties, and not a single date. Then, two months before she graduated from high school, she met Troy Tenzer. A clean-cut nineteen-year-old, Troy had been working for First National Bank of Oklahoma since his high school graduation. Ashmir and Sheila heartily approved of Troy. He had a responsible job at the bank, he treated them politely, and — best of all — he wanted to marry their daughter. They had spent the better part of Maryellen's senior year making it clear that marriage was the logical next step after graduation. The refrain of her parents' message echoed through the house so frequently that it eventually became her own melody. At seventeen she longed desperately for a husband. Unmarried, she would be a failure. As Mrs. Troy Tenzer, she would be a success.

Troy and Maryellen's wedding was as magical as a Disney movie: the bride in a cloud of white chiffon, the groom atten-

tive and handsome in his rented tuxedo. Their honeymoon
was a romantic week of sunbathing and snorkeling in Mexico.
Exactly nine months later, their daughter, Sophie, was born.
Troy embraced fatherhood joyfully. "He was a very loving man.
He had a good job, he was always there, he really tried to
provide for the three of us." Then, when Troy turned twenty-
one, everything changed. Maryellen still has no idea what
happened. "I don't know what it was…I'm not sure if he was
seeing another woman, or if he just got tired of me." Troy was
constantly irritable. He would arrive home from the bank grum-
bling about fellow employees; when Maryellen tried to
sympathize, he would angrily brush her aside and head for
the family room to sulk in front of the television set. He snapped
at Maryellen. He virtually ignored Sophie.

The tension in their house mounted. One evening, frustrated by his moodiness, Maryellen raised her voice. And Troy
slapped her. "I was shocked. I didn't try to fight back, I didn't
say, 'Don't do that again' — I was just in shock. And he got
The Look on his face." She shivers slightly as she recalls The
Look. Its image became very familiar to Maryellen over the
next eleven years. It meant that she was in danger. Troy's slaps
quickly evolved into punches. But it wasn't until one terrify-
ingly bizarre incident that Maryellen understood her life was
at risk. The family sat quietly at the kitchen table eating spaghetti. Maryellen took a bite; as she swallowed, Troy suddenly
pounced, grabbing her throat and squeezing with all his
strength. On his face was The Look. As she struggled to escape, the spaghetti still in her throat, she felt herself blacking
out. Choking, gagging, and trying desperately to catch her
breath, she fought to remain conscious. Troy released his grip
and sat back in his chair, watching her struggle. When she

finally got her breathing under control, he blandly remarked, "That was interesting. I always wondered what you'd look like when you were dying." Then he turned back to his plate, reached for his fork, and took another bite of spaghetti.

Maryellen had been taught that marriage in the Baptist church was marriage for life. Divorce was not only unsanctioned, it was unthinkable. Although Ashmir had never hit Sheila, her parents had surely fought bitterly over the years. Nevertheless, they had remained together. How could she go to them now and admit that her husband was hurting her? Surely she must somehow be at fault. A wife's job is to make her husband happy; if Troy was unhappy, she simply had to think of ways to make him happier. "So whatever I thought he wanted me to be, I tried to pretend to be that way. I tried never to argue with him. I tried to always pick his favorite foods." Troy wasn't a drinker, he didn't use drugs, so Maryellen could never predict when the violence would erupt. "He would just come home and, without any provocation at all, would start punching me or bouncing me on the wall. He'd have that same crazed look in his eyes, and a sort of 'sneer-smile' on his face. The Look."

I interrupt to ask if Troy was ever violent towards Sophie. No, she replies; if Sophie had ever been in danger, she is quite sure that she would have left immediately. But Troy never touched their daughter. In fact, he seemed to lose all interest in her. He no longer took her to the playground, sang her favorite songs, or read her bedtime stories. As a result, the only real comfort and security that Sophie and Maryellen had was one another. They became, and remain to this day, extremely close.

During those years, Maryellen remembers always feeling afraid. She was afraid when Troy was away, because she never knew what state he'd be in when he came home. She was afraid when he was at home, because she never knew when she might do or say something to trigger his attacks. As the family bread-winner, Troy always made sure his wife and daughter were provided for financially. Maryellen often focused on this one positive aspect of Troy's character as she struggled to explain her marriage to herself. "He was still what I considered to be a good man. I used to tell myself that he just had these unusual tendencies to want to hit me. Anytime I showed any type of anger at all, I knew I'd get beaten. So I tried not to. I tried as hard as I possibly could to subdue my emotions."

For the next three years, Maryellen lived like a recluse. She only left the house to run errands or to take Sophie to the playground. All her energy went into keeping the peace with Troy. When Sophie started elementary school, though, Maryellen hesitantly suggested that she find a job. Pleased with the thought of the extra income, Troy approved. Maryellen found work immediately: as a technical trainer at an Okla-homa-based insurance firm. Computers had begun to proliferate in the insurance industry, and employee training was becoming a high priority. The job required Maryellen to travel across the state, training data entry clerks and claims processors on the new computer systems. Because these sys-tems were constantly being upgraded, and because Maryellen proved to be an excellent trainer, she was eventually on the road once or twice a month. She didn't like leaving Sophie, but welcomed the opportunity to get away from Troy. For five or six days a month, she could remember what it felt like to be safe.

Meanwhile the violence at home continued, each episode worse than the last. Troy broke Maryellen's arm. He broke her nose three times. He broke three of her teeth. He ripped out big chunks of her hair. He broke two of her ribs. He broke her toe. He ruptured one of her kidneys. "And that doesn't include the verbal abuse he put me through constantly. The verbal abuse, I think, was the worst thing he did to me, because that's the only part I still struggle with after all these years." Maryellen became the world's most inspired storyteller. Each time she arrived at work with a fresh injury, she had a fresh new explanation to accompany it. Telling the truth never felt like an option; to admit that her husband beat her would have let everyone know that she was a fraud and a failure. Besides, she reasoned to herself, it wasn't as though Troy was violent every day. Months would go by with relative peace in the house. They would take Sophie to the movies. They would treat themselves to dinner at an elegant restaurant. They would spend summer weekends on their boat. Most men who batter are not physically violent every hour of the day and night, for the simple reason that they don't have to be. Over time, Maryellen learned to anticipate Troy's needs. She saw to it that he always got everything he wanted, even before he had to ask for it.

Incredibly, she was able to keep the facade of their marriage intact for eleven more years. Until the day Troy nearly killed her. "One of his co-workers had been ridiculing him, and he came home fuming. I knew I was going to get beaten, and I immediately started thinking of the excuse that I could use at work. Isn't that strange? I knew he had The Look on his face, and I knew he was about to hit me, and all I could think about was 'What am I going to tell my friends tomorrow?' I could see through the window that it was icy outside, so I had pretty nearly decided to say I had slipped on the ice." That's the last Maryellen remembers about the beating. Troy beat her until she lost consciousness, and then he got into his car and drove away. Their closest neighbor, who had heard Maryellen's screams on other occasions but had been reluctant to get involved, watched through her living room window until she was sure Troy was gone. Then she dialed 911. By the time the police and ambulance arrived, Maryellen wasn't breathing.

Maryellen lay in a coma for two weeks. Her CAT scan showed multiple brain hemorrhages. She was not expected to live; if she did survive, her doctors warned, she would suffer permanent brain damage. "While I was in the coma, I got these images of every path that I had ever been on, and how one of the paths that led me to Troy had steered me away from other paths I could have taken. And I saw what I really wanted to do and be in life. I was so far from it, but I somehow knew that I was going to do a lot of good in the world because of the terrible stuff I had been through. I never talk about this, because I can't prove it, but I saw events in the future — and some of them have come true. I'm not sure what I believe about so-called 'near death' experiences. A scientist would scoff and say it's caused by brain chemicals. A metaphysicist would probably tell you it's a vision of the afterlife. All I can say is that nobody can judge what the experience is except the person who has actually gone through it. I can't explain it, but I do know that I was not the same person after that experience. I was not."

And then, quite suddenly, Maryellen woke up. Troy was in her hospital room, in abject misery. He was horrified at what he had done. He assured her that he would never hurt her again. Everything would be different now. Everything would be wonderful. He kept talking — until he looked into her eyes. His mouth dropped open and he backed up against the wall. What he saw in her eyes was something he had never seen before: the look of willpower. "When I woke up and saw him, I knew that I didn't deserve what he had been doing to me for all those years. It wasn't right, it wasn't my fault, and there was no way I'd ever want to be around him again. At the same time, while I hated his actions, I didn't hate him as a person. I had enormous compassion for him."

Maryellen calmly and quietly told Troy what was going to happen next. She wanted him out of her life. He could have everything: the house, the boat, the bank accounts, and the stock portfolio. All she wanted was her IRA — about $25,000 — and full custody of Sophie. Troy quickly agreed; he knew a good deal when he saw one. The morning of their divorce was the last time they saw each other. As Maryellen left the court-house, she turned and said to Troy, "I never want to see you again. If you ever come near Sophie or me, you'll be sorry." Maryellen isn't sure what she meant by her threat. Would she have called the police? Would she have attacked him? All she knows is that she was filled with power, and that Troy saw it. "I think it would be best if you left the country," Maryellen told him. And he did. Troy moved to the Canadian Rockies, where he works as a river-rafting guide. Maryellen and Sophie haven't seen him in ten years.

Now that Maryellen was safe, she began the arduous and time-consuming business of putting her life back together. Her first priority was her fourteen-year-old daughter. Maryellen was deeply concerned that Sophie would carry the trauma of her mother's abuse into her own relationships with men. She found a therapist who specialized in family violence and arranged for Sophie to attend weekly counseling sessions. These continued until she graduated from high school and left home to attend college. Maryellen put herself into therapy, as well, and began to reclaim her sense of who she was and who she could be. It wasn't easy. She sometimes cried; she often had doubts. What if she couldn't make it on her own? What if she really was as worthless as Troy always said she was? Nevertheless, as time passed she gradually became stronger. For the first time in years, she was able to make eye contact. "Before, I think I never thought I was good enough to look somebody in the eye. I was very shy, very introverted, but all that changed after the divorce."

She also began a period of religious study at a local seminary. "I had left the Baptist church long ago, thinking that there was nothing for me there. I still believed in God, but I did not believe in religion, and mine certainly hadn't protected me." Still, the vision she had while she was in the coma made her want to learn more about the world's religions. It also made her curious: did other dying people have similar experiences? Her curiosity led her to the seminary's training program for bereavement counseling, where she discovered that she had a real talent for working with terminally ill patients and their families. She decided to take what was left of her savings and go back to school. "I was especially interested in bereavement counseling, because of the vision I'd had that I'd be working with people who were dying."

Maryellen's first job as a bereavement counselor was at a hospice. She found her work there enormously fulfilling. She brought a lot of relief to her patients, just by letting them talk about their fears. "It was a good experience. It felt like I was one step closer to being a doctor. But I still never quite believed that I'd go to medical school. Not until I met my present husband." Maryellen met Jake Landowski three years after her divorce from Troy. They met at the hospice, where he volunteered on Saturday afternoons. "I did not want a relationship! My daughter and I were happy. She was in college, I was successful in my new career, and I wasn't at all interested in dating." Jake, however, was in love — and extremely persistent. They kept running into each other: at the Hospice, at church, at local fund-raisers. Each time they saw each other, they'd talk. Eventually, Maryellen agreed to go out with him. About a year later, "...seeing what a wonderful person he was, how good-hearted he was, it turned out that I was the one who proposed! I never thought I'd ever trust a man again. But I trusted Jake."

Maryellen and Jake just celebrated their sixth wedding anniversary. They have very little money: they live in a small rental house, share a single car, and limit their evening entertainment to an occasional movie. These days, their finances are stretched even further. A year ago, at age forty-two, propelled by both her own dreams and Jake's encouragement, she entered medical school.

Maryellen has finished her tuna sandwich. She checks her watch; it is time for her to leave the conference room. Her afternoon will be spent with the mothers and infants who come to the Well Baby Clinic, here at the University of Louisville School of Medicine. In her white coat, with a stethoscope in her pocket, she looks more like an experienced physician than a first-year medical student. "You're going to be a great doctor," I tell her as we shake hands again. She looks me straight in the eye and smiles. "I already am a great doctor."

❧ Reflection ❧

In an abusive relationship, good values become bent and warped. Consider the value of privacy. In a healthy family, privacy is appropriate and necessary. "It's none of anybody's business that Daddy never wears pajama bottoms," we might tell a first-grader before he marches importantly off to his first show-and-tell. "In our family, we don't go around telling everybody our business."

There is a significant difference, though, between privacy and secrecy. It is highly unlikely that Sophie ever whispered the secret of her father's violence to a sympathetic teacher. Maryellen spent a significant amount of energy sustaining her family's secret, inventing outlandish stories to explain her bruises and broken bones to her co-workers. I imagine her sitting in the emergency room or the doctor's office, her attention focused, not on her latest injury, but on how she would explain that injury the next morning at the office. Her job was the one place where Maryellen was treated with respect. How shaming if her colleagues knew what she endured at home. I never breathed a word of Melvin's abuse to my fellow schoolteachers. There is a significant difference, though, between Maryellen's situation and my own. In my case, there was no external evidence of Melvin's violence. He would direct his punches at my midsection, never at my face. In Maryellen's case, her colleagues must have known that her injuries came from her husband. How could they not have known? Yet they chose to say nothing.

Her co-workers probably thought they were doing Maryellen a favor by pretending to believe her fictions, pretending that her family's secret was invisible. They must have imagined that they were sparing her feelings. And, to some extent, they were. Yet I can't help but wonder what would have happened if Maryellen's supervisor had spoken to her privately, frankly, nonjudgmentally. Would an outsider's interest have helped Maryellen see her situation more realistically? Or would it simply have embarrassed them both?

I honestly don't fault Maryellen's colleagues for their failure to speak up. It is only in the past two or three years that the general public has been educated about and sensitized to the pervasiveness of domestic abuse. The same is true for another group: the health professionals who treated Maryellen for eleven years. The frequency and nature of her injuries would have flashed like neon signs. Yet nobody asked. She would tell her internist's nurse that she had twisted her wrist, for the third time that year, playing catch with Sophie. The nurse would smile sympathetically as she wrapped the wrist in an ace bandage. She would tell the emergency room physician that she had broken her nose by walking into her bedroom door when she got up in the middle of the night to urinate; he would nod impatiently, patch her up, and send her home with Troy.

Intervention is, I acknowledge, never easy. But failure to intervene entwines victim and observer in a conspiracy of silence, distorting privacy into secrecy. Melvin and I had been married nearly two years when I tore the cartilage in my right knee. This was in 1968, long before the magic of arthroscopic surgery, so I spent a week in the hospital and came home with a three-inch scar on a knee ballooned to the size of a cranshaw melon. A few days later, I lay on the sofa, my leg elevated on three fat cushions. Slightly groggy from pain medication, I made the mistake of dozing off while Melvin was in mid-sentence. The next thing I knew, he had grasped my foot and twisted my leg with all his strength. The pain was excruciating; I shrieked uncontrollably. Suddenly our apartment door burst open. Our upstairs neighbor, hearing my screams, had come to rescue me from what he supposed was a burglar or a rapist. He stopped, frozen, at the tableau in front of him. No burglar. No rapist. Nobody here but us chickens. And here's the clincher. The neighbor looked, not at me, but at Melvin. He stammered an apology for having intruded and left the apartment nearly as rapidly as he had arrived...though with considerably less drama.

The message Maryellen received from her colleagues and physicians, the message I received from my neighbor, was crystal clear. Keep your family matters secret. Don't tell us what's really going on, and we won't ask. That way we can all pretend that everything is wonderful. That way nobody has to take any action. "If you suspect a woman in your congregation is being abused, you must not turn away," I challenge a group of rabbis at a domestic violence awareness seminar. The hands go up immediately. What if they are wrong? What if she is embarrassed? What if they speak to her and she still does nothing? These are all legitimate concerns. But they must be balanced against the message that an abused woman most certainly receives whenever a witness turns away. I may not have left Melvin sooner if my upstairs neighbor had called the police. But I wish I could reach a hand back into the past and, like a puppeteer, pull hidden strings, turning his head to face me. "Is your husband hurting you?" I would have him say. Not helping. Witnessing. The simple act of naming what he had seen would have been enough.

∞

A critical feature of Maryellen's story is that Troy was extremely violent. An abused woman is in greatest danger from
a violent partner in the first six months immediately after she
escapes. This is because domestic violence is not about anger,
but about power and control. When a woman walks out on a
batterer, she is sending a clear message that he no longer con-
trols her. Some men, faced with the realization that they have
lost control over their victim, will try to destroy her. Tragically,
too many succeed. Since Troy had already demonstrated that
he was capable of inflicting serious injury, Maryellen may have
instinctively sensed her risk. Possibly, had she tried to escape
earlier, Troy would have murdered her.

Waiting eleven years may have saved Maryellen's life. It
may also have ensured that, when she finally did leave, she
would not only survive but also thrive. During the eleven years
of Troy's abuse, Maryellen was quietly getting stronger. Until
her daughter Sophie started school, Maryellen rarely left the
house. Isolated, her only sense of herself came from the man
who was invested in keeping her under his control. Once she
went to work, though, her world expanded to include super-
visors, clients, and fellow employees. She formed friendships.
She experienced success.

Perhaps Troy's violence escalated in response to Maryellen's
growing self-confidence; perhaps, had she quit her job, she
would have saved herself a few broken bones. I find it impressive that Maryellen continued to work.

It is also significant that Maryellen's job regularly took her
out of Troy's orbit. Imagine living in a tiny house in the middle
of the woods. A strong deadbolt secures the front door; heavy

curtains shroud each window. Should a stranger attempt to peer into the house, people and objects inside will be perceived only dimly. For those inside the house, the curtains block out light, keeping the interior dark and murky. They also prevent the inhabitants from seeing how things are done in the outside world.

After living in this house for a while, you forget that there ever was a time when your world was light and sunny. Your entire reality is bounded by the walls of this house. Now and then an outside breeze moves a curtain aside, allowing you to view your surroundings with more clarity. If this happens enough times, you begin to remember what your life used to be like before you lived in the house. And one day you open a window and slip out.

For a few days each month, Maryellen had the chance, figuratively and literally, to leave her house. For a few days each month, she had breathing space; a quiet time to collect herself and know peace.

Like Maryellen, my years with Melvin were not years of unrelieved misery. I was often buoyantly happy. When I saw a look of sudden understanding and enthusiasm in the face of one of my third-grade students. When I browsed for hours in the house plants section of my favorite nursery. When I bought a basket of fragrant peaches at the Farmer's Market. I have a natural bent towards optimism, and was happy far more often than I was miserable. It's just that none of my happy times were connected with Melvin.

Occasionally it would strike me that my happiest hours were the hours I spent alone. But you don't leave someone because he makes you unhappy, any more than you drop out of a physics class because it's boring. At least, I don't. One keeps plugging along. One makes the best of things.

Melvin and I had been married for six years when he graduated from law school. His first job required him to be away from home one week out of every month. I would not have said so at the time, but I now realize how fiercely I treasured those weeks. In my imagination, I had left Melvin hundreds of times. That year, imagination became reality as I sampled life without him.

And it was good.

So I opened a window, and I slipped out.

Afterword

"Domestic Violence." A subject heading missing from most medical school curriculum outlines. A subject that no one wants to speak about, possibly for fear that others might think the speaker could be involved in such a demeaning, horrible situation. Many people place domestic violence in the same category as those other things one doesn't discuss in public (or even in private), things that change a woman's life forever: rape, teenage pregnancy, incest. Just as for rape, there are many misconceptions about domestic violence. Who is at fault? Why doesn't she get away? How could she have allowed herself to be in that situation in the first place?

In this alarming, yet riveting account of women who have survived domestic violence, Dr. Elaine Weiss raises the reader's awareness that domestic violence can be found in any intimate relationship, regardless of race, creed, or status. This is not just a problem of the poor, the uneducated, or at least the unassertive. It is clear, after reading *Surviving Domestic Violence: Voices of Women Who Broke Free*, that domestic violence is an equal opportunity employer. Most women who read this book will discover that they share at least one or two of the characteristics of the women who shared their stories with Dr. Weiss.

Chapter by chapter, story by story, Elaine Weiss dispels the myths about domestic violence and the women who survive it. In the "reflection" sections that follow each story, she gently leads the reader down the winding paths that women take to extricate themselves from their abusive situations.

This book has already impacted my life and my practice. I recently had a patient whose reaction to the significant stress of her disease made it very difficult for her to recover from the initial treatment. Her reaction was to become narcoleptic. In the course of our conversations, I learned that her first marriage had been abusive. This gave me an important insight: her reaction to stress may well be a coping mechanism that she learned while struggling to free herself from her batterer. Elaine's book enabled me to understand more about this patient and to empathize with her.

"Domestic Violence." A topic that should be part of any core curriculum for health care providers. Physicians, in particular, need to be aware of its existence and its ubiquitousness. Perhaps this knowledge will guide us to open the door or the window, even if it is just a crack, and to support these women as they take steps to break free.

Leigh Neumayer, M.D.
Director, Utah Women's Health Initiative
Associate Professor, Department of Surgery
University of Utah School of Medicine

Recommended Readings

Betancourt, Marian. *What to Do When Love Turns Violent: A Practical Resource for Women in Abusive Relationships*. New York: HarperPerennial. 1997.

Brewster, Susan. *To Be an Anchor in the Storm: A Guide for Families and Friends of Abused Women*. New York: Ballantine Books. 1997.

Evans, Patricia. *Verbal Abuse Survivors Speak Out*. Holbrook, MA: Bob Adams. 1993.

Jacobson, Neil and Gottman, John. *When Men Batter Women: New Insights into Ending Abusive Relationships*. New York: Simon & Schuster. 1998.

Jones, Ann and Schechter, Susan. *When Love Goes Wrong: What To Do When You Can't Do Anything Right*. New York: HarperPerennial. 1992.

Koppelman, Susan (Ed.). *Women in the Trees: U.S. Women's Short Stories About Battering and Resistance, 1839-1994*. Boston: Beacon Press. 1996.

Levy, Barrie and Giggans, Patricia Occhiuzzo. *What Parents Need to Know About Dating Violence*. Seattle: Seal Press. 1995.

Miller, Mary Susan. *No Visible Wounds: Identifying Nonphysical Abuse of Women by Their Men*. New York: Ballantine Books. 1995.

Wilson, K.J. *When Violence Begins at Home: A Comprehensive Guide to Understanding and Ending Abuse*. Alameda, CA: Hunter House. 1997.

About the Author

Elaine Weiss holds a doctorate in instructional design from Teacher's College, Columbia University. She is the author of two books about humanizing technology in the workplace: *Making Computers People-Literate* and *The Accidental Trainer*. After more than twenty years as an educational consultant in the business world, she began directing her considerable skills as a professional communicator toward writing and teaching about domestic violence.

Since 1994, Dr. Weiss has conducted dozens of domestic violence training sessions around the country, speaking to business leaders, social workers, health care providers, office workers, factory workers, teachers, and clergy. She has assisted with the Utah State Attorney General's "Safe At Home" program, which provides domestic violence awareness training in the workplace and the community.

Elaine has contributed to the development of three domestic violence web sites. She is a member of a national task force on domestic abuse prevention, which is currently developing a career development program to help battered women achieve economic justice. Her writings about domestic abuse have appeared in local and national publications, on domestic violence prevention web sites, and are used as teaching resources in a number of battered women's shelters.

Elaine is a Clinical Associate Professor in the Department of Family and Preventive Medicine, University of Utah School of Medicine. She welcomes comments via e-mail at eweiss@aol.com.